ADOBE® FIREWORKS® CS4

CLASSROOM IN A BOOK®

The official training workbook from Adobe Systems

www.adobepress.com

Adobe

Adobe® Fireworks CS4 Classroom in a Book®

Adobe Press books are published by Peachpit, a division of Pearson Education located in Berkeley, California. For the latest on Adobe Press books, go to www.adobepress.com. To report errors, please send a note to errata@peachpit.com. For information on getting permission for reprints and excerpts, contact permissions@peachpit.com.

Printed and bound in the United States of America

ISBN-13:   978-0-321-61219-9
ISBN-10:   0-321-61219-1

9 8 7 6 5 4 3 2

WHAT'S ON THE DISC

Here is an overview of the contents of the Classroom in a Book disc

Lesson files ... and so much more

The *Adobe Fireworks CS4 Classroom in a Book* disc includes the lesson files that you'll need to complete the exercises in this book, as well as other content to help you learn more about Adobe Fireworks CS4 and use it with greater efficiency and ease. The diagram below represents the contents of the disc, which should help you locate the files you need.

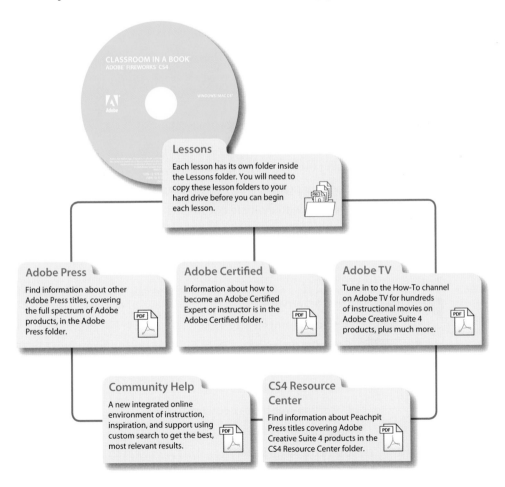

Lessons

Each lesson has its own folder inside the Lessons folder. You will need to copy these lesson folders to your hard drive before you can begin each lesson.

Adobe Press

Find information about other Adobe Press titles, covering the full spectrum of Adobe products, in the Adobe Press folder.

Adobe Certified

Information about how to become an Adobe Certified Expert or instructor is in the Adobe Certified folder.

Adobe TV

Tune in to the How-To channel on Adobe TV for hundreds of instructional movies on Adobe Creative Suite 4 products, plus much more.

Community Help

A new integrated online environment of instruction, inspiration, and support using custom search to get the best, most relevant results.

CS4 Resource Center

Find information about Peachpit Press titles covering Adobe Creative Suite 4 products in the CS4 Resource Center folder.

CONTENTS

BONUS SUPPLEMENTAL CHAPTERS 12 AND 13
ARE LOCATED ON THE COMPANION DISC

GETTING STARTED

Adobe Fireworks® is a professional imaging application that combines vector and bitmap imaging technologies and techniques in a single graphics application. This unique approach to imaging is due to the specific focus of Fireworks, which is creating and manipulating screen graphics for the web or for other screen-based tools such as Microsoft PowerPoint or Adobe Flash® Professional. Fireworks is a tool that lets you quickly and easily create, edit, or alter graphics and designs. And it's a blast to work with, too!

With the release of Adobe Fireworks CS4, the program has gained even more distinction as a unique application for *rapid prototyping*. The built-in flexibility of Fireworks and its "everything is editable all the time" mandate have been present since it was created. When creating mockups and prototypes, where client or design changes can come fast and furious, this type of flexibility is very important. Features such as multiple pages, Photoshop integration, and workflows like Flex Skinning and AIR prototyping make Fireworks an essential tool in the design process.

About Classroom in a Book

Adobe Fireworks CS4 Classroom in a Book is part of the official training series for Adobe graphics and publishing software developed by experts in association with Adobe Systems. The lessons are designed to let you learn at your own pace. If you're new to Adobe Fireworks, you'll learn the fundamental concepts and features you'll need in order to begin to master the program. And, if you've been using Adobe Fireworks for a while, you'll find that Classroom in a Book teaches advanced features, including tips and techniques for using the latest version of the application and for creating web and application prototypes. Although each lesson provides step-by-step instructions for creating a specific project, there's room for exploration and experimentation. You can follow the book from start to finish, or do only the lessons that match your interests and needs. Each lesson concludes with a review section summarizing what you've covered.

What's in this book

This edition covers many new features in Adobe Fireworks CS4, such as exporting interactive PDF files, creating AIR prototypes, wrapping text on a path, and exporting a standards-based web page mockup using CSS and HTML.

An overview of the new Adobe interface is covered in the first lesson, where you will learn how to configure the panels and document windows in Fireworks to suit your workflow. You will learn how to edit bitmap images and work with vector paths to create web interfaces. You will learn how to create and edit symbols, a powerful feature of Fireworks, and learn how Fireworks integrates with other Adobe CS4 applications like Dreamweaver, Photoshop, Bridge, and Flash.

Prerequisites

Before you begin to use *Adobe Fireworks CS4 Classroom in a Book*, you should have a working knowledge of your computer and its operating system. Make sure that you know how to use the mouse and standard menus and commands, and also how to open, save, and close files. If you need to review these techniques, see the documentation included with your Microsoft Windows or Macintosh system.

Installing Adobe Fireworks

Before you begin using *Adobe Fireworks CS4 Classroom in a Book,* make sure that your computer is set up correctly and that it meets the necessary system requirements for software and hardware. You'll need a copy of Adobe Fireworks CS4, of course, but it's not included with this book. If you haven't purchased a copy, you can download a 30-day trial version from www.adobe.com/downloads. For system requirements and complete instructions on installing the software, see the Adobe Fireworks CS4 Read Me file on the application DVD or on the web at www.adobe.com/support.

Fireworks and Bridge use the same installer. You must install these applications from the Adobe Fireworks CS4 application DVD onto your hard disk; you cannot run the programs from the DVD. Follow the onscreen instructions. If you chose not to install Adobe Bridge, you may want to go back and install it from the DVD that Fireworks came on.

Make sure that your serial number is accessible before installing the application.

Starting Adobe Fireworks

You start Fireworks just as you do most software applications.

To start Adobe Fireworks in Windows:

Choose Start > All Programs > Adobe Fireworks CS4.

To start Adobe Fireworks in Mac OS X:

Open the Applications/Adobe Fireworks CS4 folder, and then double-click the Adobe Fireworks CS4 application icon.

Copying the Classroom in a Book files

The *Adobe Fireworks CS4 Classroom in a Book* CD includes folders containing all the electronic files for the lessons in the book. Each lesson has its own folder; you must copy the folders to your hard disk to complete the lessons. To save room on your disk, you can install only the folder necessary for each lesson as you need it, and remove it when you're done.

To install the lesson files, do the following:

1   Insert the *Adobe Fireworks CS4 Classroom in a Book* CD into your CD-ROM drive.

2   Browse the contents and locate the Lessons folder.

3   Do one of the following:

- To copy all the lesson files, drag the Lessons folder from the CD onto your hard disk.

- To copy only individual lesson files, first create a new folder on your hard disk and name it Lessons. Then, open the Lessons folder on the CD and drag the lesson folder or folders that you want to copy from the CD into the Lessons folder on your hard disk.

NOTE: The CD also contains two bonus lessons and their accompanying lesson files. Chapter 12 discusses how to improve your Fireworks workflow and Chapter 13 discusses some of the more complex capabilities of Fireworks. PDFs of these two chapters are located in the Bonus Chapters folder on the disc and their lesson files are located in the Lessons folder.

Additional resources

Adobe Fireworks CS4 Classroom in a Book is not meant to replace documentation that comes with the program, nor to be a comprehensive reference for every feature in Fireworks CS4. Only the commands and options used in the lessons are explained in this book. For comprehensive information about program features, refer to any of these resources:

- Adobe Fireworks CS4 Community Help, which you can view by choosing Help > Fireworks Help. Community Help is an integrated online environment of instruction, inspiration, and support. It includes custom searching of expert selected, relevant content on and off Adobe.com. Community Help combines content from Adobe Help, Support, Design Center, Developer Connection, and Forums—along with great online community content so that users can easily find the best and most up-to-date resources. Access tutorials, technical support, online product help, videos, articles, tips and techniques, blogs, examples, and much more. To learn more about Community Help, watch this movie on Adobe TV: http://tv.adobe.com/#vi+f1612v1009.

- Adobe Fireworks CS4 Product Support Center, where you can find and browse support and learning content on Adobe.com. Visit www.adobe.com/support/fireworks.

- Adobe TV, where you will find programming on Adobe products, including a channel for professional web designers and a How To channel that contains hundreds of movies on Fireworks CS4 and other products across the Adobe Creative Suite 4 lineup. Visit http://tv.adobe.com.

Also check out these useful links:

- The Fireworks CS4 product home page (www.adobe.com/products/fireworks)
- Fireworks user forums (www.adobe.com/support/forums) for peer-to-peer discussions of Adobe products
- The Fireworks Developer Center (www.adobe.com/devnet/fireworks), where you will find tutorials, sample files, and other downloads
- Fireworks Marketplace & Exchange (www.adobe.com/cfusion/exchange) for free and commercial extensions, functions, templates, and more
- Community MX (www.communitymx.com) for additional free and commercial tutorials and samples

- Fireworks Zone—a tutorial, art, and news resource on all things Fireworks (www.fireworkszone.com)

- Fireworks Guru, the community forum where Fireworks enthusiasts share ideas, artwork, and solutions to design challenges (www.fireworksguruforum.com)

- Sarthak, the regularly updated Fireworks blog of Sarthak Singhal, a member of the Fireworks engineering team (blogs.adobe.com/sarthak)

1 GETTING TO KNOW THE WORKSPACE

Lesson overview

In this lesson, you will get up to speed on the Adobe Fireworks CS4 interface. You'll learn how to do the following:

- Set up a new document
- Open an existing document
- Draw a vector shape
- Get acquainted with the Tools panel
- Save a file
- Use the Property inspector to change attributes of a selected object
- Reconfigure the workspace
- Save a custom workspace
- Work with multiple documents in Tab view
- Use the History panel
- Navigate to Fireworks Help

 This lesson will take about 90 minutes to complete. Copy the Lesson01 folder into the Lessons folder that you created on your hard drive for these projects (or create it now), if you haven't already done so. As you work on this lesson, you won't be preserving the start files; if you need to restore the start files, copy them from the *Adobe Fireworks CS4 Classroom in a Book* CD.

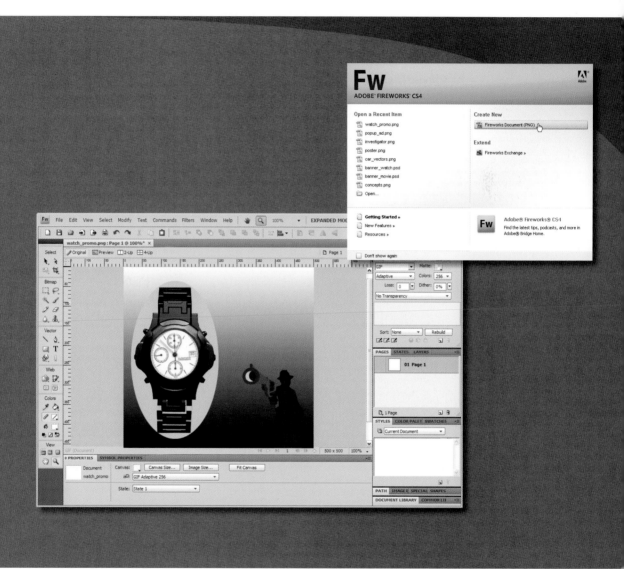

Fireworks shares a common interface with Adobe
Photoshop, Dreamweaver, Flash, Illustrator, and
InDesign. This common user interface makes it easy
to switch from one application to another without
feeling lost.

Getting started in Adobe Fireworks

Fireworks is a creative production tool, and sometimes with a creative tool, the hardest thing to do is decide where to start. We're here to help! Let's begin with a brand-new document and explore the interface in the process. As you work through this exercise, refer to the figure on page 5 to locate the main parts of the Fireworks interface.

1   Start Fireworks.

2   Choose Create New > Fireworks Document (PNG) from the Welcome screen. If you've previously changed your Preferences to not have the Welcome screen show on startup, then choose File > New.

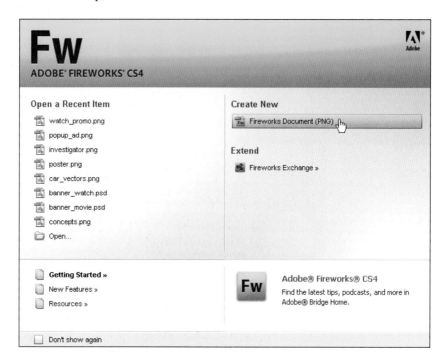

The New Document dialog box is where you set the canvas size, color, and resolution for your new design.

3   Set both the width and the height of your document to 500 (pixels). Leave the resolution and canvas color at the default settings of 72 Pixels/Inch and White, and then click OK.

The New Document dialog box closes and a new blank document opens in the Fireworks work area, as shown in this screenshot of the Windows version of Fireworks.

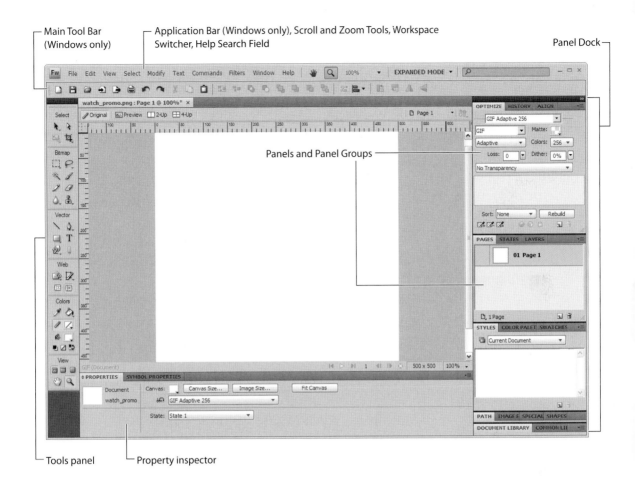

Main Tool Bar (Windows only) — Application Bar (Windows only), Scroll and Zoom Tools, Workspace Switcher, Help Search Field — Panel Dock

Panels and Panel Groups

Tools panel — Property inspector

The default workspace in Fireworks for Windows consists of the Application bar and the Main toolbar at the top of the screen, the Tools panel on the left, and open panels in the Panel Dock on the right. When you have multiple documents open, the default way to display them is as multiple tabs on one document window but you can choose to have them displayed as individual floating document windows if you prefer. The Fireworks user interface is very similar to the ones used in Adobe Illustrator, Adobe Photoshop, and Adobe Flash, so learning how to use the tools and organize the panels in one application means that you'll know how to use them in the others.

The Mac version is very similar, except the Application bar is separate from the Menu Bar, and there is no Main toolbar. By default, the Mac interface is organized a little differently from the Windows interface. In Windows, all of the panels and windows that belong to an application are contained within a rectangular frame that is distinct from other applications you may have open. The area within the frame is opaque, completely obscuring any application windows which may be behind it.

It's possible to re-create this same behavior in the Mac version of Fireworks by turning on the Application frame, which is disabled by default. To enable the Application frame, choose Window > Use Application Frame (Control+Command+F). On a Mac, however, the Menu Bar is always attached to the top of the screen and can't be moved, so it's not part of the Application frame.

Menu bar ——
Application bar ——

OS X Desktop ——

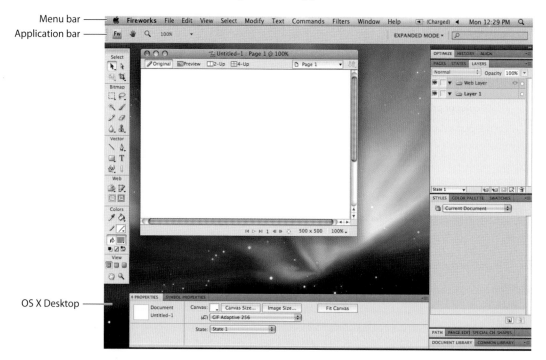

The default, on both Windows and Mac, is for new or multiple documents to be opened in tabs. If you want to detach a document for side-by-side viewing, simply drag the tab away from the tab bar and it becomes its own document window. If you prefer individual document windows, you can disable tabs in the Preferences. If the Application frame is enabled, on Windows or a Mac, you can dock numerous documents above and beside each other in what is called N-Up view.

What is the right resolution?

Pixels per inch (ppi) is a unit of measure relative only to the print world. When dealing with screen graphics, your concern should be the *pixel dimensions* (640 x 480, 760 x 420, and so on). The default resolution Fireworks begins with is 96 ppi (72 ppi on a Mac) and it can be left as is. If you are planning to use Fireworks for a print project, find out from your printer what resolution you should be using. A general guideline for print is 300 ppi. Be aware, however, that the strengths of Fireworks lie in screen graphics, not graphics intended for the printed page. For example, you cannot change the rulers to display inches—only pixels matter on the screen, so pixels are all you get for the rulers. Likewise, Fireworks does not understand or use CYMK color or printer profiles, so your end result may not print accurately.

On the plus side, Fireworks now supports PDF export, so printing your designs, for example to show to a client, etc., has become a bit more predictable.

Preparing the canvas

There are a few features we recommend setting (activating) before you start working. These features will remain set from this point forward when you create or open a new document.

1   Choose View > Rulers (Ctrl+Alt+R in Windows, Command+Option+R in Mac).

2   Choose View > Tooltips (Ctrl+] in Windows, Command+] in Mac).

Turning rulers on makes it much easier to align objects on your canvas; this is especially helpful when your work gets complex. Enabling tooltips provides you with extra information at the cursor position for the given tool being used.

Drawing a vector shape

Of course, creating shapes will be an important part of any Fireworks project. The canvas is your working area for your designs. Objects that extend outside the canvas appear clipped, but the image information is not lost; just drag the object into the canvas (or resize the canvas) to show the full object.

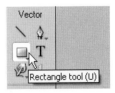

1   Select the Rectangle tool from the Vector section of the Tools panel.

2   Click the Fill color box—the one with the small paint bucket to the left of it—in the Colors section of the Tools panel to set the fill color for the rectangle. The fill color is the one that will be inside your object.

3 Using the eyedropper pointer that appears, select black from the Fill Color pop-up window. Once the color is selected, the color selector closes automatically, and the color you chose is displayed in the color box.

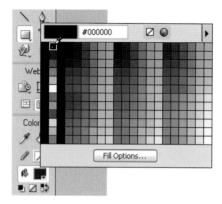

4 Bring the cursor to the upper-left corner of your canvas area. Note the small gray bubble, displaying *x* and *y* coordinates. This is the Tooltips feature at work, giving you the pixel-precise location of the cursor.

5 Position the cursor so both *x* and *y* read "0."

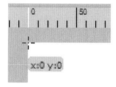

▶ **Tip:** Technically, you could accomplish everything you did here with the Rectangle tool by simply setting the background color of your new document to black.

6 Hold down the mouse button, and drag to the bottom-right corner of the canvas. The tooltip follows the cursor.

7 Let go of the mouse button when you see the coordinates match your document dimensions of 500 × 500. The rectangle will stay selected after you release the mouse. (You can tell an object is selected by the light blue border around the object, and the small control boxes at each corner.) The rectangle is a special, grouped vector object, so you won't see the blue border when it is selected (more on grouping objects in Lesson 2).

▶ **Tip:** If you didn't get an exact match for dimensions, you can tweak the vector shape's size in the Property inspector, located at the bottom of the interface. Click inside the width or height field and type the correct size. Tabbing, pressing Enter or Return, or clicking away from the field will lock any changes in place.

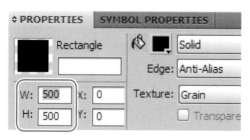

8 LESSON 1 Getting to Know the Workspace

Saving the file

Before going any further, it's a good idea to save your work.

1 Choose File > Save As.

2 Browse to the Lesson 1 folder.

3 Set the filename to **watch_promo.png**.

4 From the Save As Type field, choose Fireworks PNG.

5 Click Save.

● **Note:** Since you began with a new, untitled document, you can also choose File > Save (Ctrl/Command+S), and the Save As dialog box will still display. Because you are using Fireworks image objects (the vector rectangle), Fireworks assumes you want the new design to remain as editable as possible, and gives you the option only of saving as a Fireworks PNG file (see below). If you choose File > Save As, Fireworks gives you many more file format options to choose from.

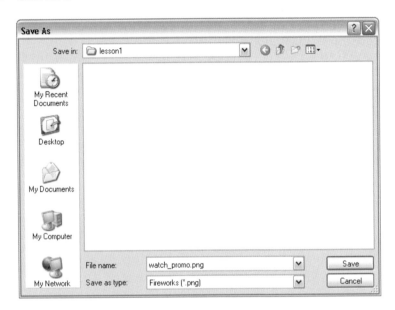

More about the Fireworks PNG format

Like many applications, Fireworks has its own native format that gives you access to all the creative options within the program—in this case, a modified version of the PNG format. As you add effects, layers, or pages (to name a few features), this information is stored within the Fireworks PNG file so that you can open and edit the file easily at any time. However, this can cause a bit of confusion for new users, because there is also a standard, flattened PNG format common to many graphics applications. When saving files, Fireworks differentiates between these "flavors" by indicating "Fireworks PNG" or "Flattened PNG" in the Save As Type field.

Using the Tools panel

The Tools panel in Fireworks is separated into six labeled areas: Select, Bitmap, Vector, Web, Colors, and View. This makes it easy to quickly identify the appropriate tool for the graphic object you plan to work on or create.

The Select tools let you select, crop, and even scale or distort objects. The main selection tool is the Pointer tool ▸.

The Bitmap tools are for editing or creating new bitmap objects. You can make bitmap selections with any one of several bitmap selection tools, such as the Magic Wand or the Marquee tool. You can do basic photo editing by using the Rubber Stamp (also known as Clone) tool, or selectively sharpen, blur, lighten, darken, or smudge pixels that are part of a bitmap image. You can paint or draw bitmap objects using the Brush or Pencil tool. The only caveat is that Bitmap tools can't be used to alter vector objects.

The Vector tools let you create or edit vector paths and shapes. As you saw in the first exercise, you can draw vector shapes on the canvas quite easily. You can use the Pen tool to create your own custom shapes or paths. Of special note is the Text tool T . Some people don't realize this, but text is actually a vector—be it in Photoshop, Microsoft Word, Fireworks, or many other applications. Vector tools can't be used to edit bitmap objects.

The Web toolset is not large, but it contains two very important tools: the mainstays of Fireworks and its ability to create interactive documents and optimize graphics for use on the web. You can create interactivity with the Hotspot tools, or take things further by creating interactive visual effects using the Slice tool. The Slice tool also allows you to optimize specific graphic elements for the web. The other two tools simply show or hide the web components on the canvas.

The Colors tools let you control Stroke and Fill colors. Remember, the roots of Fireworks are in the vector world, so you will not see Foreground and Background color options, as you would in primarily bitmap editing software like Photoshop. You can sample colors from anywhere on the desktop using the Eyedropper tool or fill a bitmap selection with color by using the Paint Bucket or Gradient tool. You can also swap the fill and stroke colors or reset the fill and stroke to their defaults.

Last are the View tools. You can toggle between three views: Standard, Full Screen with Menus, and Full Screen (no menus or panels visible). The Zoom tool and Hand (scroll) tool are at the bottom of the View toolset.

More tools than meet the eye

Take a closer look at the icons in the Tools panel. You will notice several that have a small triangle in the bottom-right corner. This indicates there are multiple tools available from within that square. You can see and use the other tools by clicking and holding the icon.

The three shapes at the top of this list are *vector primitives*, or basic shapes. Everything below the dividing line falls into the category of special vectors called Auto Shapes; they are controlled "under the hood" by JavaScript and are great for creating many common but complex vector shapes without the need of any drawing skills.

With the document we worked on previously open, do the following:

1   Click and hold the Rectangle tool in the Vector tool area. A tool menu pops up.

2   Select the Ellipse tool.

3   In the Tools panel, set the Fill color to light gray from the Color Picker.

When you hold down the Rectangle tool icon, you see this list of all the common vector shapes Fireworks has to offer.

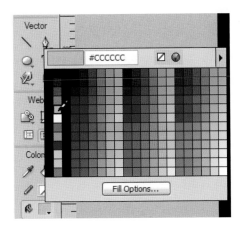

4   Move the cursor onto the canvas, and draw an oval (ellipse) that is 231 pixels wide by 401 pixels high.

5   Select the Pointer tool, and reposition the ellipse to an *x* and *y* value of 20 and 50, respectively.

6   Save the file.

What's a primitive shape?

The word *primitive* borrows the same definition used in many 3D modeling applications: *a geometric form or expression from which another is derived.* In other words, the Fireworks *Primitive* tools provide a start toward building shapes of your own.

Using the Property inspector

As you select different tools, the Property inspector will update and display editable attributes for the selected tool. The Property inspector is context sensitive, and will also change based on the active selection on the canvas.

As we saw in the first exercise, it was pretty easy to find and add a rectangle shape and change its fill color using the Tools panel. When a shape is selected, you can change many other vector attributes in the Property inspector.

1   In the Property inspector, choose Gradient > Linear from the Fill Category menu (next to the Fill Color box). The vector ellipse's fill color changes to a gradient.

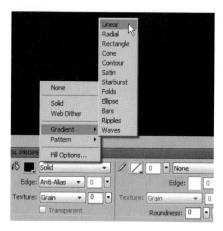

Next, you will set the colors for the gradient.

2   Click the Fill Color box to launch the Edit Gradient pop-up window. The top swatch sliders (little black boxes) control the opacity of the gradient. The swatches underneath the gradient allow you to change or add colors. You can ignore them for now, though, as we're going to keep this nice and simple.

3   Click the Preset combo box and select the White, Black preset.

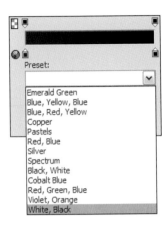

The gradient fill now runs vertically, starting with white at the top and fading to black at the bottom.

4   Try changing the gradient colors manually by clicking the small color swatches. To add other colors, just click the mouse somewhere along the gradient preview and choose a color for the new swatch.

5   When you're done, click away from the Edit Gradient pop-up window to close it.

6   Save the file once again.

● **Note:** Feel free to experiment with the other Fill categories, but remember to come back to the black-and-white gradient before continuing with the lesson.

▶ **Tip:** There are many cool—and free—command panels for Fireworks; these are generally referred to as extensions. One very nifty extension for Fireworks is the Gradient panel. You can learn more about it at www.adobe.com/devnet/fireworks/articles/gradient_panel.html.

Configuring panels and panel groups

Your computer monitor is one of those places where you're always trying to *make more room*. No matter what size the screen is, we designers always want more room to build our designs. A fair portion of the interface is taken up by panels by default. Panels are controls that help you edit aspects of a selected object or elements of a document. Each panel is draggable, so you can group panels in custom arrangements.

Many panels are visible by default in an area on the right side of the interface called the panel dock. A *dock* is a collection of panels or panel groups displayed together, usually in a vertical arrangement. Resizing the docked panels is one way to quickly make more room for your design.

You can group and ungroup panels by dragging them into and out of the existing panel groups docked to the side of the screen.

By default, the dock is in Expanded Mode, in which the foremost panel in each group is fully expanded so you can see its features. Collapse individual panel groups by clicking once on the empty area of the gray tab bar.

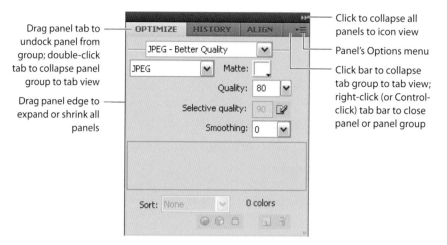

Drag panel tab to undock panel from group; double-click tab to collapse panel group to tab view

Drag panel edge to expand or shrink all panels

Click to collapse all panels to icon view

Panel's Options menu

Click bar to collapse tab group to tab view; right-click (or Control-click) tab bar to close panel or panel group

A glance at the Application Bar at the top of the interface will show the current workspace configuration in the Workspace Switcher. You can quickly reduce the dock width by choosing a different workspace.

1   Select the Workspace Switcher and choose Iconic Mode. All panels collapse, and the dock narrows to display only panel icons.

2   Click any panel icon. The panel group expands, and the chosen panel becomes active.

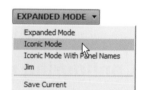

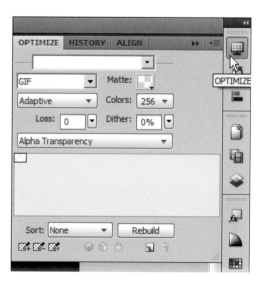

3 Click the panel tab (or the double arrow icon) to return the group to its collapsed state.

▶ **Tip:** You can also quickly collapse the dock by clicking once on the black strip at the top of the dock.

4 Position the mouse over different icons to see a tooltip of what panel each icon represents.

5 Choose Iconic Mode With Panel Names from the Workspace Switcher. This setting makes the docked panel groups wider, but not nearly as wide as the default Expanded Mode. If you want to free up desktop space and aren't sure of the tools icons, this mode might just be perfect for you.

Customizing panel arrangements

It's very easy to arrange the panels and panel groups in a configuration that helps you work faster. For example, some designers like to be able to see both the Pages and Layers panels at the same time. In this exercise, you will separate the Pages panel from its current panel group.

1 Switch back to Expanded Mode.

2 Drag the Pages panel's tab just above the panel group. A blue highlighted drop zone appears. Release the mouse button; the Pages panel forms its own group, just above the Layers and States panel group.

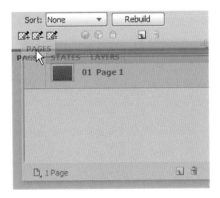

● **Note:** You can access all the available panels in Fireworks by choosing the desired panel's name from the Window menu. In some cases, these panels will appear floating above the design.

3 Drag the States panel's tab to the right of the Layers panel's tab. Notice how easily they just slide across each other.

▶ **Tip:** You can also collapse the Property inspector by clicking on the empty area of the tab bar.

Creating custom workspaces

In addition to taking advantage of the existing preset workspaces, you can configure the workspace specifically to help you work the way that's best for *you*. You can also save these customized workspaces so that you can quickly switch from a compact mode to a dual-screen mode or even just a custom panel view that holds the panels you would use most often.

To create a custom workspace, set the panels you wish to see, at the desired size and visibility.

1 Go to the Workspace Switcher.

2 Choose Save Current. A dialog box will appear where you can name the new workspace arrangement.

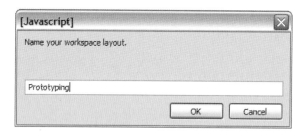

3 Name the workspace and click OK, or click Cancel if you don't want to save the configuration. If you save the workspace, it will appear in the Workspace Switcher from this point onward.

Deleting a custom workspace

While it's easy to *make* a custom workspace, it's not so easy to *delete* it. There is no way to remove a custom workspace within the Fireworks interface. You can overwrite the workspace by changing the panel setup and then saving the new workspace with the old name, but you're still stuck with the workspace.

To remove a custom workspace, you will need to go to Application Data\Adobe\ Fireworks CS4\Commands\Workspace Layouts in Windows or ~/Library/Application Support/Adobe/Fireworks CS4/Commands/Workspace Layouts/ (where "~" represents your Home folder) and delete the JSP and XML files associated with your custom workspace.

Working with multiple documents

Before we finish this lesson, let's have a look at the Fireworks CS4 Document window features. When you have more than one file opened, the Document windows for each are tabbed and easily accessible.

1 Choose File > Open, and browse to the Lesson 1 Folder from the CD.

2 Ctrl-click (Windows) or Command-click (Mac) to select the watch.png and investigator.png files.

3   Click the Open button. If you haven't changed your Preferences from the
    defaults, all three files are now open in Fireworks and you can access each one
    by clicking on the appropriate tab at the top of the document window.

Creating a floating document window

Tabbed documents function much like the tabbed panels. You can drag them to
change the tab order. You can even drag a tabbed document out from the tab bar
to float it.

1   Click and hold on the watch.png tab, and drag it away from the other tabs.
    When you let go, it becomes a floating window.

    Document-arrangement options don't stop there, however.

2   Drag the watch.png file to the right side of the main document window until
    you see a blue highlight appear.

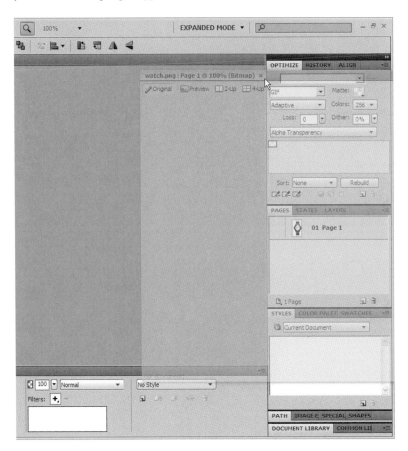

3 Release the window; you now have two sets of docked document windows. You can have as many files as you like docked in this manner.

Both floating and docked windows support tabbed documents.

4 Select the investigator.png file, and drag its tab over to the watch.png window.

5 Move the file so the cursor appears in the tab bar. You will see that familiar blue drop-zone indicator again. Release the file; it is now tabbed with the other document window.

Dragging and dropping between floating windows

With the watch_promo.png file now separate from the other two files, it's easy to drag and drop the watch and investigator images onto the canvas area of the promo file.

1 Select the Pointer tool (black arrow) from the upper left of the Tools panel.

2 Click to select the artwork in the investigator file, and drag it over to the promo design.

▶ **Tip:** Not only does Fireworks support layers and sublayers, just like Photoshop, but for even more control over your design structure, you can also have multiple objects in a single layer.

3 Position the image at the bottom of the design, near the right.

4 Release the mouse button.

If you look at the Layers panel, you will see the new image has been added to the current layer.

5 Select the watch.png file, and use the Pointer tool to drag the watch from its own canvas to the promo canvas.

6 Position it near the left middle for now. The watch_promo.png file should look something like the figure below. Adjust the positioning as necessary, and save the file.

● **Note:** Because Fireworks moves so seamlessly between vector and bitmap artwork, you probably didn't even realize that the investigator file was a vector object!

Undoing steps

Being able to go back in time is an all-important feature of most software. Fireworks gives you a couple of ways to undo an error. Undo is, of course, the tried-and-true, familiar method.

1 Press Ctrl+Z (Windows) or Command+Z (Mac). The last step you made will be undone.

2 Press Ctrl+Z/Command+Z three more times. This will take you further back in the history of the document.

3 Press Ctrl+Y (Windows) or Command+Y (Mac). This will reapply the last undone step.

Another option exists, though: the History method.

1 Select the History panel from your grouped panels or choose Window > History.

2 Drag the History slider (left of the panel) downward until it can go no farther. This should bring you back to the point where both the watch and the investigator images are visible in the promo document.

3 Drag the slider up, and watch the promo canvas. As the slider reaches each previous step, you will see your documents change.

Creating custom commands with the History panel

Do you find yourself doing the same things over and over again in a file (or multiple files)? Save your history steps as a custom command, which you can then use again any time, from the Commands menu. This can eliminate some of your repetitive but necessary drudge work.

To save a custom command, simply select all the steps you need in the History panel, and then click the small floppy-disc icon in the lower-right corner of the panel. You will be prompted for a name. Make it short but relevant; it's the name that will appear in the Commands menu.

The History panel doesn't record mouse movements, so in order to get a complete custom command, use the keyboard commands and menu items.

Review questions

1 What is the importance of the Tools panel?

2 How do you collapse panels and why would you?

3 If you can't find a panel in the workspace, how can you locate it?

4 How does the Property inspector help when you are working on a design?

5 Where can you find out more about the Fireworks interface?

Review answers

1 The Tools panel is where all the selection, editing, and creative tools are located. From cropping an image to scaling it, whether retouching or building vector objects or adding interactive elements, everything you need begins in the Tools panel.

2 Panels can be collapsed by choosing a different workspace, or by clicking on the dark gray bar at the top of a panel group. This can free up a significant amount of room in your workspace, letting you see more of your design without having to zoom out as much.

3 To open a panel, choose Window > [panel name], or press the panel's shortcut (listed in the Window menu).

4 The Property inspector is a context-sensitive panel, changing its options as you select different tools or various objects on the canvas. The Property inspector makes it easy to alter tool and object attributes from one handy location.

5 Pressing F1 will launch the Adobe Community Help website. You can also select options from the Help menu or search for a specific topic using the Search field in the Application Bar.

2 WORKING WITH BITMAP IMAGES

Lesson overview

If content is king on the web, then graphics are the king's finery.
Everyone enjoys surfing through a good-looking, organized website or
using a professionally designed interface. Adobe Fireworks includes a
solid set of tools for creating and editing bitmap images. As you work
through this lesson, you will learn how to do the following:

- Select and use some of the bitmap tools in the Tools panel

- Open and import bitmap images in Fireworks

- Use a variety of methods to crop images

- Set options for a selected tool using the Property inspector

- Use guides to help position and align images

- Use the 9-slice Scaling tool to scale bitmap images

- Use various bitmap tools and filters to adjust brightness, contrast,
  and tonality of bitmap images

- Correct images using the Rubber Stamp tool

- Align objects on the canvas using the Align panel

This lesson will take about 90 minutes to complete. Copy the Lesson02
folder into the Lessons folder that you created on your hard drive for
these projects (or create it now), if you haven't already done so. As
you work on this lesson, you won't be preserving the start files; if you
need to restore the start files, copy them from the *Adobe Fireworks CS4
Classroom in a Book* CD.

Everyone enjoys surfing through a good-looking,
organized website or using a professionally designed
interface. Adobe Fireworks includes a solid set of tools
for creating and editing bitmap images.

Resolution and file size

Image resolution and file size are directly related to each other. The greater the number of pixels in an image, the larger the file size will be. We're not talking about the printed size of an image here; we're dealing specifically with the number of pixels that make up an image. For example, many current digital cameras will capture an image consisting of 3000 pixels horizontally by 2000 pixels vertically (or greater). Do the math, and you'll quickly see that an image with this resolution contains 6 million pixels in total and weighs in at about 23 MB.

The higher the capture resolution, the larger the file size will be.

Image resolution vs. image quality

Resolution and *quality* are two different things; you can have a high-resolution image that actually doesn't look very good, due to poor quality in the original scan or heavy image compression that might be set on a digital camera. *Resolution* refers to the actual number of pixels that make up the image, not the empirical or subjective quality of the image.

Tips for working with bitmaps

Good-quality graphics are key assets to many professional websites. The image-editing and layout tools in Fireworks give you the freedom to do most—if not all—of your bitmap work without leaving the application.

That said, there are a couple of caveats to keep in mind:

- The maximum canvas-creation size in Fireworks is 6000 x 6000 pixels. You can work on files that are larger than this, but 6000 x 6000 pixels is the largest that you can create within the program.

- Fireworks was designed to work with graphics destined for screen use, and it's here that its speed and flexibility really shine. While you can open and work on very high-resolution files in Fireworks, you may find the application begins to get sluggish over time. And you may not want to have several of these files open at the same time.

Cropping an image

Cropping is a common way to remove extraneous detail, letting you focus more exclusively on a specific part of an image. In this exercise, you will remove surrounding detail in a photo to help focus on just the actor's face.

1   Choose File > Open, and browse to the file Mark_actor06.jpg in the Lesson02 folder on your hard drive. Click Open.

2   Select the Crop tool from the Tools panel.

3   Click and drag a box around the face of the actor. Include the hat and part of the tie.

4   Press Enter or Return to crop the image.

Hmm, looks like we got a bit too close to the collar. We'd better go back.

5   Press Ctrl+Z (Windows) or Command+Z (Mac) to undo the crop.

6   Making sure the Crop tool is still selected, draw the crop one more time, leaving a bit more space on the sides.

Note: Notice the small square boxes at the corners and middle of each crop line. These are control handles, which let you alter the crop's dimensions before committing to it.

7 Move the cursor to the middle control handle on the bottom of the image, and drag it upward. Stop when the crop line touches the upper red stripe in the actor's tie.

8 Press Enter or Return to commit to the crop.

9 Choose File > Close, and don't save the file when you are prompted.

Cropping a single bitmap image in a design

Cropping single images is fine, but what if you need to crop an image that's already on a layer in a design? Fireworks offers a way to do this as well.

1 Open watch_promo.png from the Lesson02 folder.

2 Choose 150 from the Zoom Level menu on the Application Bar to zoom in to 150%.

3 Use the Pointer tool ( ) to select the watch.

4 Choose Edit > Crop Selected Bitmap. Crop marks will appear around the watch image.

5 Drag the top and bottom crop marks so that only the watch face is inside the crop.

6 Press Enter or Return to commit to the crop.

Managing images on the canvas

When you have more than one image or object on the canvas, Fireworks gives you a variety of ways to work with those images, from showing and hiding objects to positioning and grouping them. You'll find that steps like these are a common part of most design workflows.

Adjusting the watch position

To experiment with this feature, you'll adjust the position of the watch image you've already got open. Because you are dealing with exact measurements here, you need to be aware of the exact *x* and *y* coordinates of the image.

1 Select the watch with the Pointer tool, and check the values for *x* and *y* in the Property inspector. The watch should be positioned at X: 30, Y: 135.

2 If the watch is not in position, use the arrow keys on the keyboard to move the image one pixel at a time.

▶ **Tip:** You can hold down the Shift key while pressing the arrow keys to move the selected object(s) five pixels at a time. You can also change a selected object's position by entering new values in the Property inspector.

Hiding and locking objects

With the watch cropped, there's no need for that large ellipse, so let's hide it from view for now.

1 Go to the Layers panel, and locate and select the ellipse.

2 Click the eye icon to hide the ellipse from view.

3 To ensure you don't accidentally select the now-invisible ellipse, click the lock icon.

To give the design a grittier feel, you're also going to replace the gradient backdrop with a bitmap image, so we'll set up for that now.

4 Hide the gradient object by clicking its eye icon in the Layers panel.

5 Lock the gradient object in the Layers panel by clicking the empty box beside the eye icon.

Working with guides

In this exercise, you will use guides to help ensure an exact position and height between the canvas and an image you will import into the design. Guides are great tools for aligning and placing objects on the canvas.

1 If rulers are not visible, choose View > Rulers.

2 Move the cursor to the ruler at the left of the window.

3 Click and drag toward the canvas. You will see a vertical guide appear. You will also see a tooltip appear beside the guide, with an x value. (If you don't see the tooltip, choose View > Tooltips.) This value is the horizontal position of the vertical guide.

4 When the tooltip displays 0, let go of the mouse. The guide will drop at that location.

5 Drag in another vertical guide, and place it at 500.

6 Drag guides from the top ruler to these positions: 0 and 500. If you need to reposition guides, you can simply select them with the Pointer tool and drag them to a new position. This effectively boxes in the canvas.

Importing images

A very quick way to add existing images to a design is to *import* them onto the canvas. You will add your new background image this way. Importing gives you the ability to scale the image proportionately when you add it to the canvas.

1 Zoom out to 66% using either the Zoom tool in the Tools panel or the Zoom Level menu in the Application Bar.

2 Choose File > Import.

3 Browse to the Lesson02 folder, and locate the promo_backdrop.jpg file.

4 Click Open.

Back on the canvas, you'll notice that the cursor has changed to an inverted L shape (⌐). This is the Import cursor. If you click and drag the mouse, you will begin to draw a marquee. If you release the mouse button, your image will be imported at the dimensions you've created via the marquee, based on the height to width (aspect) ratio of the original image. If you simply click the mouse button without dragging, the image will be imported at its full height and width, with its top-left corner where you clicked.

5 Place the cursor in the upper-left corner of the canvas, and then click and drag toward the lower-right side of the canvas.

   You will notice from the marquee guideline that in order to get the image to cover the full width of the canvas, it's actually going to be too tall. This will result in a portion of the image being cut off. For the purpose of this exercise, you will want the entire image to fit within the height of your canvas, regardless of its width.

6 Drag the cursor up so that the height of the image fits within the canvas area. The cursor should snap to the bottom guide when you get within five pixels of it. When you release the mouse, the image will appear, but, as noted earlier, it doesn't cover the full width of the canvas.

7 Check the Property inspector to ensure that the x and y positions of the image you imported are both at 0, and press Ctrl+S (Windows) or Command+S (Mac) to save your changes.

Distortion-free bitmap scaling

Scaling objects in one direction—whether they are bitmap images or vector shapes—can cause unwanted distortion. Take, for example, the image you just imported. Traditional scaling will distort the entire image, giving you an undesirable result. But Fireworks has a great new feature called 9-slice scaling that eliminates distortion. First let's review how it used to be.

Scaling the "old" way

1 Make sure the backdrop image is still active—look for the blue control handles at the four corners of the shape. If you don't see them, use the Pointer tool to select the image on the canvas.

2 Select the Scale tool (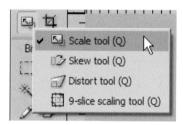) from the Tools panel.

Control handles will appear around the rectangle.

3 Drag the right-middle control handle straight out to the right side of the canvas.

4 Release the mouse button, and note how the image is stretched and somewhat distorted. It can definitely be better!

5 Press the Escape key to cancel the transformation.

Avoiding distortion with the 9-slice Scaling tool

If a bitmap image contains an area that doesn't have a lot of detail (a very important point to note), you can use the 9-slice Scaling tool to make the image fit with no noticeable damage.

1 Make sure the multiple watch image is still selected.

2 Select the 9-slice Scaling tool from the Tools panel (▣). The scaling handles appear again, but the image is now divided with special 9-slice guides. These guides can be positioned prior to scaling, and anything that is outside the guides will remain unchanged during a scaling operation.

3 Move the cursor over the vertical 9-slice guide on the left.

4 When the cursor changes to a double-headed arrow, click and drag the guide in the image to the area of fog that has no noticeable detail.

5   Position the right side 9-slice guide in the fog as well, similar to what you see below. Watch out for those puddles in the foreground of the photo! The position of the horizontal guides is not important for this example.

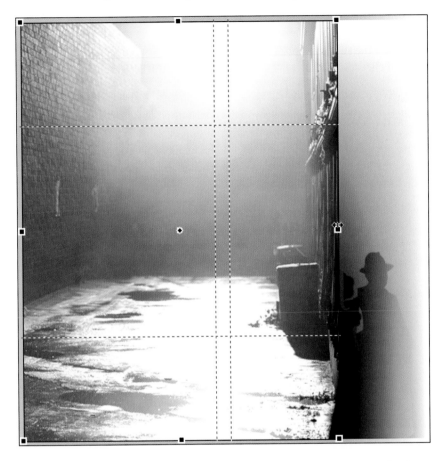

6   Drag the right-middle control handle out to 500 pixels. Tooltips do not display when using the 9-slice guides, so watch the top ruler to make sure you have reached the 500-pixel distance.

7   Release the mouse button. Only the areas enclosed by the 9-slice guides (areas with no real detail) were scaled (stretched). The sides of the image, where the puddles and garbage gave the image detail and definition, were not stretched.

    You now have an image that actually fits the canvas!

8   If the watch and investigator images are hidden by the new background, drag them up in the stacking order in the Layers panel (or choose Modify > Arrange > Send To Back to move the alley scene to the bottom of the pile of images).

9   Press Ctrl+S (Windows) or Command+S (Mac) to save your work.

Adjusting tonal range

The background image you've imported adds a certain air of mystery to the design, but it's a bit low in contrast, lacking visual impact. You will use a Live Filter to adjust the contrast.

1   Ensure the alleyway photo is selected (look for that blue bounding box), and then click the plus sign (+) in the Filters area of the Property inspector.

2   Choose Adjust Color > Levels. A histogram dialog box appears.

Notice the graph, which tells you the distribution of tones in the image. The Levels dialog box shows you the distribution of tones in the selected image; you use it to alter shadows, midtones, and highlights. Directly below the histogram are the input level sliders: shadows on the left, highlights on the right, and midtones in the middle.

In this image, you'll notice that there is nothing displaying in the histogram for the darker tones.

3   Drag the left slider to the right so that it almost lines up with the beginning of the histogram chart. Set the value to about 90, as seen here.

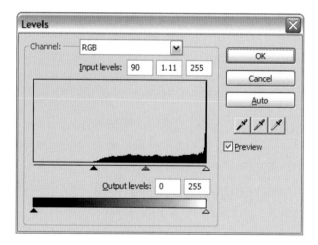

What are Live Filters?

Live Filters are nondestructive effects you can apply to most objects (vector, bitmap, or symbol) within Fireworks. The great power and advantage of Live Filters is that you can always edit the effect at a later date. If you feel the filter is too harsh, or too subtle, just click the "i" icon to edit the filter properties. Note that this icon becomes available once the Live Filter has been added to the Property inspector.

4   Lighten the midtones slightly by dragging the middle slider to the left, for an input value of 1.11. Click OK.

The Levels Live Filter now appears in the Filters list in the Property inspector.

This is definitely an improvement, but now things are a little too dark in the shadows and a bit too bright in the midtones. You will reopen the Levels filter and make further adjustments.

5   Click the "*i*" icon next the Levels filter in the Live Filters category of the Property inspector. The Levels dialog box reopens.

6   Change the shadow input value to **80** by typing the numbers into the leftmost input box above the histogram.

7   Change the midtone value back to **1** by changing the value in the middle input box. Click OK.

8   Press Ctrl+S (Windows) or Command+S (Mac) to save your work.

Using the Align panel

Guides and Smart Guides are very helpful for positioning items, but they're really "one object at a time" features. If you have multiple items you need to reposition, the Align panel is the tool to use.

In this exercise, you will add in four more watch versions, to show the available color range of the product. You can import each file one at a time if you like (tan, green, blue, and magenta_watch.jpg), but to make things a little easier for you, we have provided a single Fireworks PNG file which contains all four watches, and that is the one you will use in this exercise.

1   Choose File > Import.

2   Browse to the Lesson02 folder, and select the watch_colors.png file.

3   Click Open.

4   Click anywhere on the canvas to import the collection of images at their original sizes. You can see things are a bit messy, much like how it would look if you quickly dragged and dropped the images from another document window.

In the Layers panel, you will notice that each image is truly a separate object. This is one of the beauties of a Fireworks PNG; because each image was a unique object in the original PNG file, each is imported as a separate, unique object.

All four objects should still be selected. If not, use the Shift key and click on each watch in turn to select them all.

5   Open the Align panel (choose Window > Align if you don't see the Align panel tab in your Panel groups).

6   Click the Align Top Edge button to align the top edges of all of the objects.

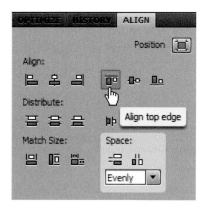

7   Change the Space menu option to a value of **10**, instead of the default option of "Evenly."

8   Click the Space Evenly Horizontally icon right above the Space menu. You now have a nice, neat, evenly spaced row of watches. Don't worry if the watches aren't all fully on your canvas; we'll deal with that in the next exercise.

9   Press Ctrl+S (Windows) or Command+S (Mac) to save your work.

Grouping objects together

The canvas is starting to fill up with several graphics. You're going to make your life a little easier by grouping that row of watches together. Grouping temporarily turns a series of selected objects into a single object, making it easier to manipulate them.

1   Make sure the four watches are still selected.

2   Choose Modify > Group.

    In the Layers panel, you will see that the four watches are now part of the same object, with a new name of Group: 4 Objects.

3   Select the Pointer tool, and, if necessary, drag the group to the left edge of the main watch. Smart Guides—the purple dashed lines that appear and disappear as you move one object around the edges of other objects on your canvas—will help you get this adjustment just right.

    The row of watches takes up a fair amount of space, overlapping the investigator image. You will scale the group to make it fit the layout better.

4   If you're not already there, zoom to 100%.

5   Select the Scale tool from the Tools panel. Because the four watch images are grouped, you will be able to scale them all at the same time.

6   Drag the upper-right corner control handle inward until the tooltip displays values of W: 344, H:80. Remember, if you don't see the tooltips, choose View > Tooltips.

7   Double-click inside the group to apply the size.

8   If necessary, use the Pointer tool to reposition the group of watches so it is aligned with the large watch, as mentioned earlier.

9   In the Property inspector, set the y position to **398**, so the group of watches is below the main watch.

▶ **Tip:** For precise scaling, choose Modify > Transform > Numeric Transform, and then choose the Resize option from the pop-up menu.

10 Press Ctrl+S (Windows) or Command+S (Mac) to save your work.

Adjusting brightness with the Dodge and Burn tools

Sometimes a photo has good general exposure, but there are areas in the image that are too light or too dark. These areas need some local adjustment, and this is where the Dodge and Burn tools come in very handy.

The Dodge and Burn tools are part of the bitmap-retouching toolset; their effects are permanent (sometimes called "destructive") in that the tools completely alter pixel values. As we go along in this exercise, you will also learn how to protect your original image.

1 Choose File > Open, and browse for the detective.png file in the Lesson02 folder.

2 Click Open.

   This image is pretty good, but the subject's face is a bit too dark, and his white shirt a bit too bright. You'll use the Dodge and Burn tools to correct this.

3 To keep your original safe, make a copy of the photo by dragging its thumbnail down to the New Bitmap Image icon in the Layers panel.

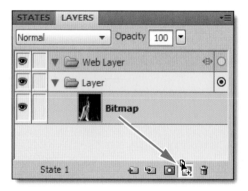

4 Double-click the word Bitmap next to the selected image in the Layers panel, and rename it **Retouch**. This will help you to differentiate between the two images with a quick glance at the Layers panel at any time.

5 Use the Zoom tool to magnify the subject's face.

Now we're ready to delve into the different uses of the two specific tools.

▶ **Tip:** Rather than adjusting the zoom level from the Application Bar or menus, and then having to reposition the image focus on the detective's face, it's easiest to use the Zoom tool to drag a marquee around the face. When you release the mouse, Fireworks automatically centers the selected area on the canvas, and you're ready to go.

Lightening with the Dodge tool

1 Select the Dodge tool from the Tools panel.

2 In the Property inspector, change the Size to **48**. Set the Edge to **100** (for a soft-edged brush), the Shape to Circular, the Range to Shadow, and the Exposure to **6**.

3 Carefully paint over the actor's face and neck without releasing the mouse. Avoid painting over the hat.
   Because you have chosen Shadows as the range, you can safely paint over the bright areas of his face without concern.

4 Press Ctrl+Z (Windows) or Command+Z (Mac) to undo the editing, and compare the original with the lightened version. The effect is subtle, but noticeable.

5 Press Ctrl+Y (Windows) or Command+Y (Mac) to reapply the dodging.

Note: Dodging and Burning are more realistic if the exposures are set to low values and then reapplied if necessary. High value can cause unwanted results. If you find the changes you're making to be too subtle, you can paint over the area a second time—or more, if you prefer.

Darkening with the Burn tool

1 Switch to the Burn tool.

2 In the Property inspector, change the Size to **33**, the Range to Midtones, and the Exposure to **6**. Leave Edge and Shape the same (100 and Circular).

3 Paint over the bright area on the actor's cheek.

   Burning in will add exposure, making the cheek slightly darker. This should give an appearance of more evenly applied lighting to the detective's face, instead of one side being significantly lighter or darker than the other.

   Now we'll alter the shirt slightly to complete the changes this image needs.

4 Set the Zoom level to 100% again.

5 Change the Size to **60**, the Range to Highlights, and the Exposure to **8**. You don't have to change the Shape and Edge settings.

6 Without releasing the mouse button, paint over the white shirt sleeve and shirt on the left side of the image. Notice how the shirt gets somewhat darker.

7 Hide the upper copy of the image by clicking its eye icon in the Layers panel, to compare the original with the altered image. Although each of the changes we made were small, the overall effect on the image is quite substantial.

8 Continue to alter the image if you like, or simply save the file by pressing Ctrl+S (Windows) or Command+S (Mac).

Tip: A quick way to get to 100% magnification is to press Ctrl+1 (Windows) or Command+1 (Mac) or simply double-click the Zoom tool in the Tools panel.

Applying the Unsharp Mask Live Filter

When resizing an image (often called *resampling*), pixels are added or removed from the file. When you resize an image to larger than its original size, you are adding pixels and increasing the file size. Generally this *upsampling* is not recommended in Fireworks unless it is only by a small percentage or for special effect, because the image quality will degrade noticeably. When you make an image smaller (*downsampling*), you are removing pixel data from the image and reducing the file size. This tends to make the image softer, but we can gain back some of the original crispness of the photo by applying a filter called Unsharp Mask. Unsharp Mask can be applied as either a permanent filter or as a Live Filter. For the greatest flexibility, Live Filters are a better option.

1 Choose File > Open, and locate the policeman.jpg file in the Lesson02 folder.

2 Select the Open As Untitled option at the bottom of the dialog box. (This will, of course, open an untitled copy of the image.)

3 Click Open.

When the file opens, you will notice it is quite large—4368 x 2912 pixels in size. This is one of the high-resolution images from the movie photo shoot and is much too large for use on the web. You will resize it to a more suitable dimension and resolution.

4 Choose Modify > Canvas > Image Size to launch the Image Size dialog box.

5 Make sure the Constrain Proportions option is checked.

6 Set the width to 600 pixels, and press Tab. The height will automatically change based on the width you have entered.

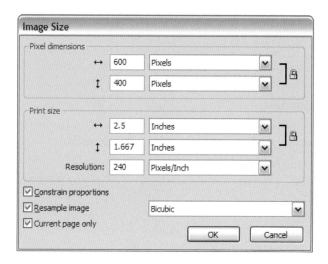

7 Click OK.

8 Click the Add Live Filters icon (+ sign) in the Property inspector.

9 Choose Sharpen > Unsharp Mask to open the Unsharp Mask dialog box. The default properties are a bit extreme for a low-resolution file, so we'll alter one slightly.

10 Change the Pixel Radius to a value of **1**.

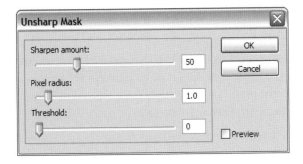

11 Deselect the Preview option to see the image without sharpening.

12 Activate Preview again. Notice how there is slightly more contrast and even a bit better separation between the officer and the background. This is because Unsharp Mask increases the contrast only of *edge pixels* (the place where a dark and light pixel meet).

13 Click OK to apply the filter.

Unsharp Masking properties

Generally, higher resolution images can handle (and sometimes need) higher amounts of unsharp-masking than low-resolution images. The three controls for Unsharp Masking are explained below.

- **Sharpen Amount:** This is listed as a percentage, and controls how much darker and lighter the edge borders become. This can also be thought of as how much contrast is added at the edges.

- **Pixel Radius:** This affects the size of the edges to be sharpened. A smaller radius enhances smaller-scale detail. Higher radius values can cause halos at the edges (a highlight around objects), making images look unnatural. Fine detail needs a smaller radius value. Pixel Radius and Sharpen Amount are reciprocal; reducing one allows more of the other.

- **Threshold:** Controls how far apart adjacent tonal values have to be before the filter does anything. The threshold setting can be used to sharpen more pronounced edges while ignoring more subtle edges. Low values have a greater effect because fewer areas are excluded. Higher threshold values exclude areas of lower contrast.

Repairing areas with the Rubber Stamp tool

Fireworks is not Photoshop. There—we've said it. If you've got large images that require major manipulation, then chances are you should do that kind of heavy-duty work in Photoshop first, as it's better suited to editing very large files. Every job has a correct tool. That said, Fireworks comes with a decent set of standard retouching tools, including the Rubber Stamp tool. These tools will handle most basic retouching requirements. The Rubber Stamp (also known as the Clone Stamp) tool copies pixel detail from one location in a photo and pastes it into another (presumably damaged or unsightly) area. Maybe there is a scratch in some packaging, or a fly-away thread in some clothing. Maybe you need to smooth out skin tones in a photo or remove an unwanted highlight in a shiny object. These are all good examples of when to use the Rubber Stamp tool.

Here are the general steps to using the Rubber Stamp tool:

- Click an area to designate it as the source (the area you want to clone).

- The sampling pointer becomes a cross-hair pointer.

- Move to a different part of the image, and drag the pointer. Two pointers appear. The first is the source and is in the shape of a cross hair. Depending on the brush preferences you've selected, the second pointer is a rubber stamp, a cross hair, or a blue circle. As you drag the second pointer, pixels beneath the first pointer are copied and applied to the area beneath the second.

> **Note:** To designate a different area of pixels to clone, Alt-click (Windows) or Option-click (Mac) another area of pixels.

Now you will test out this process. In the file we'll open, the overall image is fine, but there are some distracting wrinkles in the sofa cushion where the actor is seated. You're going to smooth over that area using the Rubber Stamp tool.

1 Choose File > Open, and browse for the mark_actor02.jpg file in the Lesson02 folder.

2 Click Open.

3 Zoom in, as described earlier in the chapter, to focus in on the cushion area. When retouching, it's always good to get close to your subject matter.

4 Select the Rubber Stamp tool from the Bitmap tools area of the Tools panel.

Notice that the Property inspector updates, displaying attributes for the Rubber Stamp tool. You can set the brush size and the edge softness of the brush (100 is soft, 0 is hard). You can also decide whether you want to keep your brush aligned with the original source of sampling and if you want to sample from all the layers/objects in your document, or just the active object.

5   Locate an area on the cushion that is mostly smooth and similar in brightness to the wrinkled area. Hold down Alt (Windows) or Option (Mac), and click to sample the pixels from this area.

6   In the Property inspector, set your brush size to **28** pixels and the edge to 100%. Leave the Opacity setting at 100.

7   Deselect the Source Aligned option. This will ensure that the sampling always begins at the same source point, no matter where you begin your actual rubber-stamping.

8   Move the cursor over to the beginning of the wrinkled area.

9   Click and hold the mouse button, begin painting carefully over the area, and continue painting until the large wrinkles are gone. Some variation in tone is fine; you want the retouching to look as realistic as possible. If necessary, release the mouse button and repeat the process to get further to the right or lower down in the wrinkles. Because the Rubber Stamp tool duplicates the exact pixels, the texture and tone of the leather remain visible.

▶ **Tip:** If you notice that the area you are cloning seems much too light or dark, stop stamping, press Ctrl+Z (Windows) or Command+Z (Mac) to undo the painting, and resample (Alt-click on Windows or Option-click on Mac) from a more suitable area.

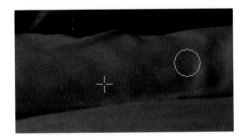

Retouching on a separate bitmap object

Cloning as described above is a permanent (destructive) process; you are literally replacing pixels in one area with pixels from another. If you save and close the file, those changes become a part of the image.

Many professionals prefer to do this type of retouching on a separate layer. In this way, they avoid the potential for permanently ruining (or even just changing) an original image. Fireworks lets you do this kind of work in an empty bitmap object, even in the same layer as the original artwork.

Look at the actor's face; he's got a couple of creases on his forehead, which make him look a little older and more tired than perhaps he really is. You are going to retouch those wrinkles as a separate object, first creating the necessary empty bit-map object. This way, you can show or hide the wrinkles, depending on your plans for the image.

An empty bitmap object is an area containing no pixel data. It gives you the opportunity to add new pixel information as a separate, unique object. Once you create this object, you must add pixel data to it in your next step, or the object will be removed from the Layers panel. You might use this object if you are planning to use the Brush or Pencil tools to add colored bitmap lines. In our case, we'll be using it as a place to hold retouching data. The beauty of this technique is that your original image is not altered in any way.

1   Open the Layers panel, and, if necessary, resize the panel so you can see all the elements. You should see the Web Layer, Layer 1, and Background. When you open a single image such as this one, Fireworks places the photo as an object on the Background layer, and also creates an empty layer called Layer 1.

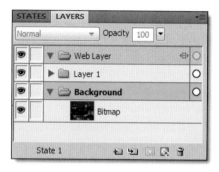

▶ **Tip:** Naming layers and objects helps you identify them as you work. While not necessary, it's a good practice to follow.

2   Select the photo in the Layers panel.

3   Double-click the name Bitmap under the Background layer, and type **photo** to rename it.

4   Click the New Bitmap Image icon (![icon]). A transparent (empty) Bitmap object will appear above the photo object.

Next, you will use the Rubber Stamp tool and the new bitmap object to take years off the actor's face.

Instant face-lift

1   Select the Zoom tool, and draw a selection around the actor's face.

2   Switch to the Rubber Stamp tool.

3   In the Property inspector, set Size to **5,** and leave the Edge set to 100% for a nice subtle blend.

4   Select both the Source Aligned and Use Entire Document options.

By using the entire document, Fireworks will sample from all visible pixels on any layer or object in the design. Left unchecked, Fireworks will sample only from the current object, which, being a new bitmap, has no actual pixels…yet.

5 Move the cursor above the top wrinkle at the left.

6 Hold down Alt (Windows) or Option (Mac) and click once to sample the skin tone above the wrinkle.

7 Move the cursor straight down until it is directly over the first wrinkle.

8 Hold down the mouse button, and begin painting carefully toward the right, following the entire wrinkle.

9 When you are happy with the result, repeat these steps to remove the second wrinkle.

10 Turn off the retouching (Bitmap) layer by clicking the eye icon beside the layer name. You will see the wrinkles return. Turn the layer back on, and the wrinkles vanish.

You might also notice a blue rectangle appear on the canvas, surrounding the retouching work. This is how Fireworks indicates a selected object.

Rubber-stamping can take a bit of practice, which is another reason to perform the retouching on a separate object. If your results aren't as good as you would like, you can just delete the bitmap object by selecting it and then dragging it to the Layers panel trash can icon, or by pressing Backspace (Windows) or Delete (Mac).

One other item of note: because you are adding additional objects to a photo, you will most likely want to save this file as a Fireworks PNG file in order to maintain the objects and their editability. In fact, if you press Ctrl+S (Windows) or Command+S (Mac) at this time, Fireworks will display a dialog box explaining the choices you have, and the repercussions of each.

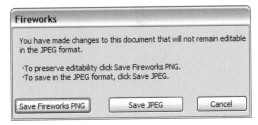

Layers *and* objects? Why?

Because the roots of Fireworks lay in the vector world—much like Adobe Illustrator—each layer can contain multiple objects. This may seem a little disconcerting if your experience is primarily with Photoshop, which is a layer-oriented application, but in fact, this *object-oriented* approach gives you much more control and flexibility over your designs. You can also create sublayers within a layer, which emulate the layer-groups workflow of Photoshop.

In the retouching workflow described in this chapter, you could just as easily have selected the empty Layer 1, added a bitmap object to that layer, and performed your rubber-stamping. It's really your choice.

Review questions

1 What is the maximum canvas size in Fireworks, and how can this affect your workflow?

2 What is the process for cropping a specific bitmap object in a design?

3 What options do you have for adjusting the tonal range of a bitmap image?

4 What are the advantages of Live Filters over traditional filters?

5 How do you use the Rubber Stamp tool, and what is a recommended workflow for using it?

Review answers

1 The maximum canvas size you can create in Fireworks is 6000 x 6000 pixels. If you have a very large file that you want to use in Fireworks, consider scaling it to more suitable dimensions before opening it in Fireworks.

2 Select the bitmap object, and then choose Edit > Crop Selected Bitmap. This will ensure that you're cropping only one object rather than the entire design.

3 If the entire image is too dark or too light, you can use the Levels dialog box to alter overall brightness and contrast. If you want to alter specific areas in the image, you can use the Dodge tool to lighten an area, or the Burn tool to darken an area.

4 Live Filters are nondestructive and completely editable at any time. Live Filters can also be applied to both vector and bitmap objects, whereas traditional filters can be applied only to bitmap objects.

5 The Rubber Stamp tool can be used only on bitmap objects, and is designed to copy pixels from one location to another, for the purpose of correcting defects or removing unwanted elements within a photo. You must first sample the area you want to use as a source by pressing Alt (Windows) or Option (Mac) and clicking on the desired area. Then you can move the cursor to the problem area and paint over it. Ideally, this type of retouching should be done within a new bitmap object, so you do not alter the original source image.

3 WORKING WITH SELECTIONS

Lesson overview

Making selections on a bitmap image is an important component of working with bitmaps. Bitmap selections isolate a specific area for alteration, protecting all other areas from being affected. For example, you might want to brighten a dark part of an image. Without a selection, this change in pixel brightness would be applied to the entire photo. In this lesson, you'll learn how to do the following:

- Make specific areas of an image active using selection tools

- Create a selection with the Magic Wand tool

- Adjust the edge of a bitmap selection

- Apply corrective filters to a selection

- Make complex selections using the Lasso and Magic Wand tools

- Modify a bitmap selection

- Save a bitmap selection for future use

- Deselect a selection

- Convert a bitmap selection to a path

 This lesson will take about 60 minutes to complete. Copy the Lesson03 folder into the Lessons folder that you created on your hard drive for these projects (or create it now), if you haven't already done so. As you work on this lesson, you won't preserve the start files. If you need to restore the start files, copy them from the *Adobe Fireworks CS4 Classroom in a Book* CD.

Making selections on a bitmap image is an important component of working with bitmaps regardless of the software application.

About selecting objects and selection tools

The bitmap selection tools are very helpful if you want to alter or copy a specific area of an image. You must also be clear on the difference between selecting an object and making a bitmap selection.

When you click on an object in the Layers panel, or use the Pointer tool to click on an object on the canvas, you are selecting (or activating) the entire object, allowing you to move, copy, or cut that object from the design, without affecting anything else on the canvas. A bitmap selection differs in that you are selecting a specific part of a bitmap image, rather than the entire object. Once selected, you can only copy or edit the area within the selection border.

Bitmap selection tools: a primer

The selection tools in Fireworks include the Marquee and Oval Marquee tools, the Lasso and Polygon Lasso tools, and the Magic Wand tool.

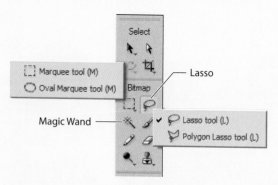

Choose the selection tool most suitable for the job. Use the Marquee (▢) or Oval Marquee (○) tool to select regularly shaped areas. Simply click and drag to draw out one of these selections after choosing the appropriate tool. Holding Shift will constrain the rectangular marquee to a square and the oval marquee to a circle.

One of the Lasso tools (the standard Lasso ○ or the Polygon Lasso ○ tool) may be better suited to select irregular areas when you make a freehand selection. The standard Lasso Tool allows you to draw a selection on the canvas using a mouse or stylus. You outline the selection by clicking to plot points around the area you want selected. You can hold down Shift to constrain Polygon Lasso marquee segments to 45-degree increments. To close the polygon selection, either click the starting point or double-click in the workspace.

If the area is full of similar shades of colors, the Magic Wand tool (◹) may be your best choice to quickly create a selection. The Magic Wand tool selects pixels based on color. If you have an area of similarly colored pixels in your image (a blue sky, for example), the Magic Wand can quickly select that part of your image. You start the selection by clicking the wand cursor on an area of your image. The wand selects contiguous pixels of the same color range, based on the Tolerance setting in the Property inspector. You can increase the tool's sensitivity by changing the Tolerance setting to a higher value.

Options

Most of the bitmap selection tools have the option to set the selection edge to Hard, Anti-alias, or Feather. A Hard edge will give you a jagged, pixelated selection. Anti-alias blends the selection with the area outside the selection, and Feather creates a softer, less accurate, blended edge selection. Unlike the other two edge settings, you can apply a pixel value to Feather to increase the blend between the inside and outside of the selection.

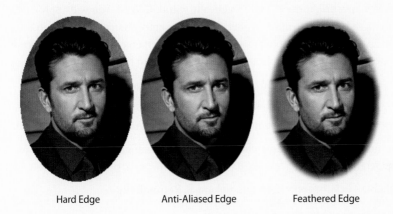

| Hard Edge | Anti-Aliased Edge | Feathered Edge |

Additional selection features for the marquee

If you choose the Rectangular or Elliptical Marquee, the Property inspector offers you additional options:

- **Normal** creates a marquee in which the height and width are independent of each other.
- **Fixed Ratio** constrains the height and width to defined ratios.
- **Fixed Size** sets the height and width to a defined dimension, in pixels.

Using Live Marquee

The Live Marquee feature is available for the bitmap selection tools listed above. By default, it is active (selected) in the Property inspector. Live Marquee gives you immediate control over the edge of your bitmap selection after it has been drawn. You can choose Hard for an aliased, hard-edged selection; Anti-alias for a softer, slightly blended selection edge; or Feather for a very soft blend. When you choose Feather, you set the amount of feathering you want. This amount will gradually blend any effect applied to the bitmap selection on both the inner and outer edges of the selection.

Selecting and modifying with the Magic Wand tool

In this section, you are going to use the Magic Wand tool to select a part of the scene in order to apply an exposure adjustment. You have some prep work to do before you can fix the image.

Getting started

1 Choose File > Open, and browse to the Lesson03 folder.

2 Select Backdrop02.jpg, and then click Open.

   Notice how bright the sky is—practically without detail. You will apply a bitmap filter to a bitmap selection, which will permanently change the pixels in the image. When you are going to apply permanent changes to a bitmap object, it's a good idea to create a duplicate of the image first, so the original is not damaged.

3 Select the Pointer tool, and click on the image to make it active.

4 Press Ctrl+Shift+D (Windows) or Command+Shift+D (Mac) to create a clone of the image. Notice that you now have two bitmap images in the Layers panel.

5 In the Layers panel, double-click the bottom bitmap image name, and change it to **Original**.

6 Double-click the top image, and rename it **Retouching**.

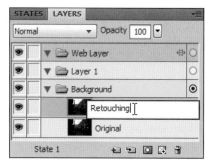

Creating the selection

Now you will create the selection using the Magic Wand tool.

1 Select the Magic Wand tool ( ) from the Tools panel.

2 Move the cursor over the sky portion of the image, and click once. As illustrated here, a selection appears.

3 In order to see how our alteration blends with the rest of the photo, choose View > Edges (or press Ctrl+H on Windows or Option+F9 on Mac). This hides the selection from view but still lets you perform actions on it, such as applying filters.

4 Choose Filters > Adjust Color > Levels.

5 Set the Shadow (Minimum Intensity) value to **20**.

6 Set the Midtone (Gamma) value to **.4**, and leave the Highlight value at 255. You can do this by typing into the input boxes or dragging the middle sliders themselves.

7 Toggle the Preview checkbox off and on again repeatedly to see how the cloud definition has changed, and then click OK to apply the filter.

● **Note:** When applying a filter adjustment to a selection, you must use the main Filters menu. You should also create a copy of the image before you begin.

▶ **Tip:** It's a good idea to zoom in on the area you are selecting to ensure a more accurate selection.

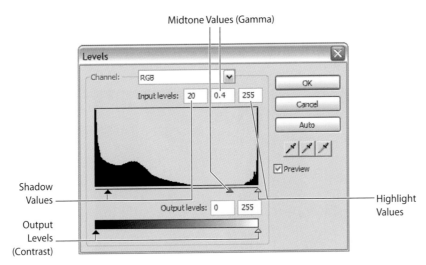

8 Save and close the file.

Using the Magic Wand tool with keyboard modifiers

Because the Magic Wand tool selects based on contiguous pixel color, sometimes areas you want included don't become part of your original selection. In this case, you can use modifier keys to add to the selection.

In this exercise, you are going to use the Magic Wand tool to select the parts of the actors' faces in order to apply an exposure adjustment. You will also modify the selection by applying a feathered edge.

1   Choose File > Open, and browse to the Lesson03 folder.

2   Select actors_together.jpg, and then click Open.

Notice the skin tones on the left cheek of the man. They're almost washed out. A similar problem exists with the woman's face. You will be applying a bitmap filter to a bitmap selection, which will permanently change the pixels in the image. When you are going to apply permanent changes to a bitmap object, you should create a duplicate of the image first, so the original is not damaged.

3   Select the Pointer tool, and click the image to make it active.

4   Press Ctrl+Shift+D (Windows) or Command+Shift+D (Mac) to create a clone of the image.

5   If necessary, select the Magic Wand tool ( ) from the Tools panel.

6   In the Property inspector, set the Edge to Feather, input a value of **4**, set the Tolerance to **32**, and make sure the Live Marquee option is selected.

7   Move the cursor to the bright area of the detective's cheek, and click once. A selection appears.

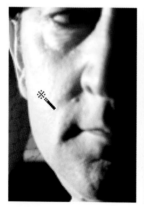

Notice that the other bright areas on the woman (her cheek and nose) are not part of the selection. This is because these areas are separated by pixels that are much darker and of different colors, and not within the Tolerance setting of the tool. Increasing the Tolerance is not the answer, either, because we would end up selecting more areas than we want for this adjustment.

8 Hold down the Shift key, and click on the bright part of the woman's cheek, between her ear and her eye.

9 Hold down the Shift key one more time, and click on the bright side of the bridge of her nose. You now have three separate selections.

10 Choose Filters > Repeat Levels. (This option is available for the last filter applied, as long as you have not restarted Fireworks.)

11 Set the Gamma Slider to a value of **.6**.

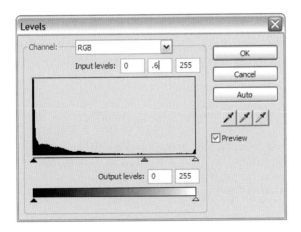

12 Click OK to apply the filter. You'll see that the skin tones of the actors' faces look much more even and are no longer washed out.

If you create a particularly complex selection, such as the one you've just done, you might want to save your efforts as an alpha channel in order to reuse the selection at a later time. See the sidebar "Saving and restoring bitmap selections." (Your file is currently in the perfect position to use these bitmap-selection functions.)

Finally, it's time to finish up with this file.

13 Choose File > Save.

Fireworks recognizes that this altered image has properties that are not supported in a flat JPEG file, so you will see a dialog box asking you for a decision about which type of file you'd like to save. If you want to retain the editability of the file, you need to save it as a Fireworks PNG file. If the original image and the bitmap selection are not important, you can opt to save the file as a flat JPEG.

● **Note:** To subtract from a selection, hold down the Alt (Windows) or Option (Mac) keys. These modifiers work with the Rubber Stamp, Lasso, Marquee, and Oval Marquee tools.

▶ **Tip:** Sometimes the marquee itself can get in your way. You can quickly show or hide the marquee by pressing Ctrl+H (Windows) or Option+F9 (Mac).

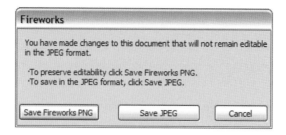

14 Click Save Fireworks PNG. This will maintain the selection information and both bitmap images. The Save dialog box will appear.

15 If necessary, browse to the Lesson03 folder.

16 Name the file **actors_together_retouched.png**, and click OK.

● **Note:** If you had chosen File > Save As, Fireworks would assume you want to save the file as a JPEG. There's a warning message in the Save As dialog box; pay attention to it! Some people don't notice the warning and later reopen their file only to learn the edits have been flattened in, and the original unaltered image has been lost. Make sure you click on the Save As Type options and choose the format you prefer.

Saving and restoring bitmap selections

Once you've created a complex selection, you can save it, giving you the option to deselect it, work on other parts of the image, and come back to that selection later. These functions are available regardless of the selection tool you've used in the first place. To save a selection, of course, you first need to have an active bitmap selection.

1 Choose Select > Save Bitmap Selection.

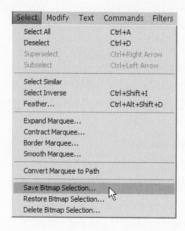

2   In the Save Selection dialog box, change the name to **cheek**.
    Leave all other settings as they are.

3   Click OK.

    Once a selection is saved, you can then call it up any time you need it
    during your session. If you save the file as a Fireworks PNG file, the selection
    remains with the file and can be restored even after the file has been closed
    and reopened.

● **Note:** If you have more than one saved selection, you can choose the correct one
from the Selection menu in the Restore Selection dialog box. In the current exercise, the
"cheek" selection is the only one in the list.

4   Press Ctrl+D (Windows) or Command+Shift+A (Mac) to deselect the bitmap
    selections on the canvas (so that you can see how to restore it).

5   Choose Select > Restore Bitmap Selection.

6   Click OK. The selection reappears on the canvas.

Selecting with the lasso tools

Selection tools are also interchangeable; you might start with the Magic Wand tool,
for example, but then use the Lasso tool ( ) to refine a selection.

1   Choose File > Open, and browse to the Lesson03 folder.

2   Open the file called Mark_actor07.jpg.

3   Create a clone of the image by selecting the image with the Pointer tool and
    pressing Ctrl+Shift+D (Windows) or Command+Shift+D (Mac).

4 Select the Magic Wand tool once again.

5 Set the Edge to Anti-alias, the value to **0**, and the Tolerance to **32**, and make sure the Live Marquee option is selected.

6 Click on the gray cinderblock wall.

7 Hold down the Shift key, and click on other areas of the wall. Avoid clicking the shadow of the detective, as this will also select parts of the gun.

8 Keeping the Shift key pressed down, click the dark segment to the right of the actor.

9 Select the Lasso tool.

10 Holding down the Shift key, draw around a large part of the shadow. Avoid lassoing the gun. You do not have to do this in one operation; indeed, it's a very good idea to zoom in for the more detailed areas.

As long as you hold down the Shift key, you can add to the existing selection. If you select an area by accident, you can switch to the Alt (Windows) or Option (Mac) key and draw around the unwanted area.

When you are done, everything except the detective should be selected.

● **Note:** Creating this selection took some time, so it's a good idea to save the selection as you did with the previous document (choose Select > Save Bitmap Selection).

11 Choose File > Save.

12 Click Save Fireworks PNG.

The Save As dialog box appears.

13 If necessary, browse to the Lesson03 folder.

14 Name the file **Mark_actor07.png**. Because you are using a different file type, you can still keep the same filename.

15 Click OK.

Other selection options

Select Inverse

Select Inverse is used to toggle the active selection between the original selection and the non-selected areas.

Sometimes, selecting the unwanted part of the image is easier.

Let's say you have a photo of city scene with a clear sky in the background. You want to do some levels or filter adjustments to the city area. It will be easier (and faster) to use the Magic Wand tool to select the evenly colored sky. Then you can use Select > Select Inverse to reverse the selected areas, making the city scene the active selection.

Select Similar

Select Similar will add to the current bitmap selection, based on colors within the active selection. Anywhere the colors within the selection appear throughout the image, they will become part of the new selection. Select > Select Similar can be used with any bitmap selection.

Modifying a selection

You can expand, contract, or smooth any active bitmap selection by choosing the desired action from the Select menu.

Converting a selection to a path

In Fireworks, you can easily convert bitmap selections to vector paths. Paths can be easier to edit than bitmap selections, because you aren't as likely to delete an entire path by accident. If you are adjusting a bitmap selection and forget to use the Shift and Alt (Windows) or Option (Mac) modifier keys, you can easily delete the entire selection.

1   If the selection is not active, choose Select > Restore Bitmap Selection.

2   Choose Select > Convert Marquee To Path.

    The selection is removed, and in its place is a new path object, filled with the last attributes used for vector objects.

3   Select the Pointer tool, if it's not already selected.

4   Choose Pattern > Light Panel from the Fill Category menu in the Property inspector.

5   Choose File > Save.

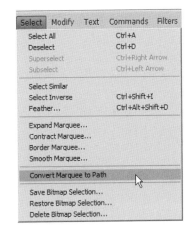

If you look at the Layers panel, you'll see that Fireworks shows the Light Panel as a composite path in the preview of the document, as shown here.

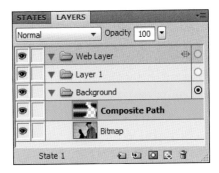

You will learn much more about working with paths in Lesson 4.

Review questions

1   What is the difference between selecting objects and making bitmap selections?

2   What are the five bitmap selection tools in Fireworks, and what are their functions?

3   What does the Tolerance setting do when you're using the Magic Wand tool?

4   What are the two keyboard modifiers you can use in conjunction with the bitmap selection tools?

5   How do you create a clone of a bitmap image? Why would you do this?

Review answers

1   When you click on an object in the Layers panel or use the Pointer tool to click an object on the canvas, you are selecting (or activating) the entire object, allowing you to move, copy, or cut that object from the design, without affecting anything else on the canvas. A bitmap selection differs from this in that you are selecting a specific part of a bitmap image, rather than the entire object. Once selected, you can copy or edit only the area within the selection border.

2   The Fireworks selection tools are the Marquee and Oval Marquee tools, the Lasso and Polygon Lasso tools, and, finally, the Magic Wand tool.

Typically, you use the Marquee or Oval Marquee tool to select regularly shaped areas, and the Lasso or Polygon Lasso tool to select irregular areas. You use the Magic Wand tool to select pixels based on color. While drawing the initial selection, the Shift key constrains the marquee tools to symmetrical objects (squares and circles) and the Polygon Lasso tool segments to 45-degree increments.

After a selection has been created, holding the Shift Key can be used to add to the selection. Holding the Alt (Windows) or Option (Mac) key lets you subtract from a selection.

3 The Magic Wand tool selects contiguous pixels of the same color range based on the tolerance setting in the Property inspector. You can increase the tool's sensitivity by changing the Tolerance setting in the Property inspector to a higher value.

4 The Shift key is one, and the Alt (Windows) or Option (Mac) key is the other. Both of these modifiers work with the Rubber Stamp and freehand Lasso tools, as well as the rectangular and elliptical marquees. Holding down the Shift key lets you add to an existing selection. To subtract from a selection, hold down Alt (Windows) or Option (Mac).

5 To clone a bitmap image (or any other object), press Ctrl+Shift+D (Windows) or Command+Shift+D (Mac), or choose Edit > Clone to create a clone of the image. Creating a clone of your original image lets you edit and retouch a cloned image without damaging the original.

4 WORKING WITH VECTOR GRAPHICS

Lesson overview

Using vector tools is pretty intuitive, but to the new user, they may seem a bit intimidating. In Fireworks (similar to Illustrator or Flash), you can draw almost any shape at all by using vectors. Now is your chance to familiarize yourself with several vector tools, including vector shapes and the Pen tool. You will also use the Property inspector and Subselection tool to modify vectors you've created. In this lesson, you'll learn how to do the following:

- Draw simple vector shapes
- Use guides to place objects on the canvas
- Learn the differences between vector and bitmap images
- Use the 9-Slice Scaling tool to scale vector shapes
- Learn how to use Auto Shapes
- Create paths with the Pen tool
- Edit paths with the Pen and Subselection tools
- Create a custom shape
- Customize the fill and stroke of a vector shape

 This lesson will take about 60 minutes to complete. Copy the Lesson04 folder into the Lessons folder that you created on your hard drive for these projects (or create it now), if you haven't already done so. As you work on this lesson, you won't preserve the start files. If you need to restore the start files, copy them from the book's CD.

Vectors are a powerful component of Fireworks,
giving you the flexibility to create unique custom
shapes or call on the many pre-built vectors that are
part of Fireworks.

About vectors

Computer drawings that use mathematical equations to draw lines and fills onscreen are known as *vectors*. A vector is simply the path between two defined points on the screen, with properties such as color and thickness applied to the path.

Fireworks comes with a range of prebuilt vector shapes, most of which are found in the Tools panel in their very own section. There is also a series of special prebuilt Auto Shapes that can be found in the Shapes panel.

The most commonly used vector tools are the Text, Shape, and Pen tools.

● **Note:** Most designs contain elements to hold other objects such as text and graphics, and when standard shapes aren't enough, you can turn to the Pen tool to create your own custom vector shapes or paths.

Basic vector drawing techniques

The Tools panel contains several basic vector shapes, which include the Line tool, the Rectangle tool, the Ellipse tool, and the Polygon tool. (You've already worked with the Rectangle tool; take a moment to review "Drawing a vector shape" in Lesson 1.) As you already know, to create one of these shapes, select the appropriate tool, and then click and drag on the canvas. These basic shapes can be scaled, skewed, and distorted using the Transform tools in the Tools panel. You can use the Property inspector to change the fill and stroke and even add a texture for a more realistic look.

● **Note:** Text is also a vector, but you are focusing on shapes in this exercise.

With a bit of practice you'll be creating your own custom vector shapes and masks before you know it. But we'll start off simply, by adding a couple of vector shapes to the watch_promo.png file you worked with in Lessons 1 and 2, and then altering those shapes, and learning how to use guides for better precision in placement.

Deleting shapes

In Lesson 1, you created an ellipse. In Lesson 2, you hid and locked it. Now you'll delete it.

1 Choose File > Open, and navigate to the Lesson04 folder.

2 Select the watch_promo.png file, and click Open.

3 Click the lock icon next to the ellipse in the Layers panel to unlock the object.

4 If it's not already selected, select the ellipse in the Layers panel.

5 Drag the layer to the Delete Selection (trash can) icon in the Layers panel.

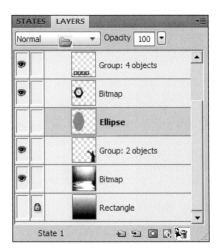

Adding guides

Guides are great tools for aligning and placing objects on the canvas. To help with placement of the new shape, you will set up guides on the canvas.

1 If rulers are not already visible, choose View > Rulers.

2 Move your cursor over the left ruler.

3 Click and drag toward the canvas. You will see a vertical guide appear. You will also see a tooltip appear beside the guide, with an x value. This value is the horizontal position of the vertical guide.

4 When the tooltip displays 19, let go of the mouse. The guide will drop at that location.

5 Drag another vertical guide, and place it at 255.

6 Drag guides from the top ruler to these positions: 125 and 362. If you need to reposition guides, you can simply select them with the Pointer tool and drag them to a new position.

● **Note:** Tooltips are visible only if View > Tooltips is selected.

▶ **Tip:** If you want a higher degree of accuracy, double-click on the guide; you will then be able to set the location numerically.

Measuring distances between guides

Once guides are drawn, you can easily measure the distance between guides.

1 Place your cursor over the watch.

2 Hold down the Shift key. Note the distances that appear along with dashed lines and arrowheads (areas highlighted in red in the following figure). These are guide measurements, and they can be invoked any time you have guides on the canvas. The guide dimensions should be 236 x 237 pixels.

3   Move the cursor around the canvas. The guide measurements will update based on the nearest guides.

Placing an object using guides

Once guides have been placed, you can accurately draw the new shape, so long as objects are set to snap to guides.

1   Choose View > Guides, and make sure that Snap To Guides is checked.

2   Select the Rectangle tool from the Tools panel.

3   Move the cursor onto the canvas, near the upper-left intersection of the guides that box in the large watch. Click and drag to draw a rectangle. When you come within five pixels of the guides on the right and bottom, the rectangle will snap to those guides, giving you an exact dimension, placed exactly where you want it to be.

4   Before releasing the mouse, press the Up Arrow key four times. If you pay close attention to the rectangle you are drawing, you will see the corners become rounded.

5   Release the mouse. The shape will appear, with all of the Fill properties that were used last. It will also cover the watch.

6 In the Property inspector, set the Fill Category to Solid and the color to medium gray (#999999).

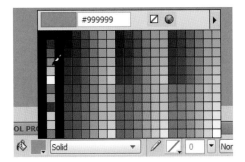

7 If necessary, expand the Layers panel so that you can see both the new rectangle and the watch layers.

8 Double-click on the new rectangle name, and change it to **watch background**.

9 Drag the watch background object below the watch in the Layers panel to change the stacking order.

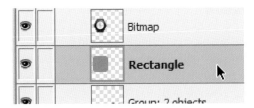

Resizing vectors

Early in the creation of the watch_promo.png file, you added a grouped vector shape in the form of a silhouetted detective pointing a rather exaggerated gun. You are going to resize this vector object, with the added side benefit of seeing how this resizing affects—or doesn't affect—the quality of a vector.

1 Select the detective silhouette using the Pointer tool.

2 Select the Scale tool, and drag the object inward from any corner to make it proportionately smaller.

3 Press Enter or Return to accept the new size. Note that other than the reduced size, the object does not appear damaged or altered. The edges and overall shape have not been distorted.

4 Select the Scale tool again.

5 Drag the upper-left corner of the scale handles up and to the left, until the tooltips read w:250, h:369.

w:250 h:369

If you had treated a bitmap image in this manner (sizing down, and then sizing up beyond the original size), the image quality of the bitmap would have decreased noticeably. The edges could become jagged and the image itself would become pixelated. This vector shape, however, remains undamaged.

Changing the appearance of basic vector shapes

As mentioned earlier, you can scale, skew, and distort basic vector shapes using the Transform tools in the Tools panel (look at the tools hidden under the Scale tool), and you can change their fill, stroke, color, and even texture using the Property inspector. In this section we'll concentrate on basic modifications.

1 Select the gray rectangle you created in the previous exercise.

2 In the Property inspector, change the Fill Category from Solid to Pattern > Paint Blue.

3 Below the Fill Category menu, choose Onyx from the Texture menu.

4 Adjust the amount of the texture to 40%.

5 Still in the Property inspector, from the Stroke Category menu, choose Dashed > Dash Double.

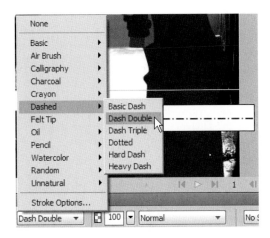

6 Set the stroke color to Black from the color picker in the Stroke section.

7 Set the Tip Size to a value of **2**. The end result should be similar to what you see below.

8 In the Layers panel, make sure the detective object is stacked above the rounded rectangle. This creates a sense of depth in the design, as the detective object now slightly overlaps the rectangle.

Feel free to try other textures and strokes. If the stroke is heavy enough, you can even add a texture to it to further enhance the effect.

Bitmap and vector graphics: What's the difference?

The intrinsic ability of Fireworks to move back and forth between vectors and bitmaps—and even combine both graphic types—makes it a very powerful creative tool. But it's important to understand the differences between these two types of graphics, so you can know which is the right kind to use in any situation.

As the name implies, bitmap graphics (also referred to as "raster") are made of a specific number of pixels "mapped" to a grid. Each pixel has a specific location and color value. The greater the number of pixels, the higher the resolution of the image and the larger the file size. If you resize a bitmap image, you are either adding to or taking away pixels from the image, and this will affect image quality and file size. The initial number of pixels in a bitmap image is set at the time of capture (when taking a digital photo, or scanning an image, for example).

Vector graphics are, simply put, mathematical equations describing the distance and angle between two points. Additional information, such as the color and thickness of the line (stroke) and the contents of the path (fill), can also be set. Unlike bitmap graphics, vectors can be resized up or down with no detrimental impact to the vector shape itself.

Another example of the differences between vector and bitmap is this: A photograph can accurately depict a physical scene in a single image layer. To produce similar realism in a vector illustration could require hundreds and hundreds of vector shapes stacked upon each other.

This is not to suggest that bitmaps are better than vectors, or vice versa; both of these main graphic types are integral to visual communication.

Scaling vector objects

In Lesson 2, we talked about how scaling—whether for bitmap or vector shapes—can cause unwanted distortion, and how the new 9-slice Scaling tool eliminates that problem. Because this is such a useful tool, and because it's a bit different for vectors, we'll practice with it again, this time scaling the rounded rectangle in the watch_promo.png file to make it large enough to hold the text that you will be adding to the design.

Remember, traditional scaling will distort the corner radii of this rectangle, giving you an undesirable result. Let's try this first to see what happens.

Scaling the "old" way

1   Make sure the rectangle is still active; look for the blue control handles at the four corners of the shape. If you don't see them, use the Pointer tool to select the shape on the canvas or in the Layers panel.

2   Select the Scale tool (🔲) from the Select section in the Tools panel. Control handles will appear around the rectangle.

3   Drag the top middle control handle straight up by 60 pixels. Refer to the tooltips as you drag the handle.

4   Release the mouse, and note how the corners of the rectangle have been distorted. (If the guides or the rectangle's bounding box are obscuring your view of the corners, click Preview on the Document window, but be sure to click back to Original to continue working.)

5   Press the Escape key to cancel the transformation, or press Ctrl+Z (Windows) or Command+Z (Mac) to undo the scaling if the rectangle is no longer active or if another tool was selected.

Distortion-free vector scaling with the 9-slice Scaling tool

Now let's see how big of an improvement we can get with the new method.

1   Drag in a guide from the top ruler, and position it at 64 pixels. (Tooltips do not display when using the 9-slice Scaling tool, so this is necessary in order to set an accurate height.)

2   Select the 9-Slice Scaling tool from the Tools panel. As in the last exercise, the scaling handles appear again, but the image is now divided with special 9-slice guides. The default settings are fine in this case.

● **Note:** 9-slice guides can be positioned prior to the scaling operation; anything outside the guides' four corners will remain unchanged.

3 Drag the top middle control handle straight up to the guide. Note that the corners do not distort this time.

4 Double-click inside the object or press Enter or Return to accept the rectangle's new dimensions.

Adding text to your design

Images and text go together in many designs. In this exercise, you will add a call-to-action tagline to the design.

1 Select the Text tool.

2 In the Property inspector, choose a showy, bold font family (we chose Broadway).

3 Set a large font size. For Broadway we chose 24 points; if you are using another font, start at 24 and see if that size works for you.

4 Set the Fill Color to Black.

Text engine integration

Fireworks now uses the same text engine as Illustrator and Photoshop, so copying and pasting text from these applications, or opening a Photoshop file containing text, has become much more predictable. Prior to CS4, Fireworks used its own proprietary type engine to render fonts. If you open a Fireworks CS3 or earlier source PNG file, Fireworks CS4 will prompt you to update the fonts in the file. This is recommended, but you may have to reposition your text areas once the update has been completed.

5   Type **See the Movie**.

6   Press Enter or Return, and then type **Get the Watch**.

If you find the spacing between your letters is too narrow, you can set the tracking to a higher value. Tracking adjusts the space between two adjacent characters, and is Fireworks' method for manual kerning (spacing) of letters.

7   Use the Pointer tool to select the text box.

8   Change the tracking value to alter the distance between letters. Using the Broadway font, we adjusted the tracking to a value of 40.

9   Set the font's weight to bold. If the font has multiple families, you can do this in the Font Style menu in the Property inspector. If the font doesn't have any derivatives, you can apply faux bold by clicking the B icon.

10 Use the Pointer tool to position the text area so it is centered left to right within the rectangle. A Smart Guide will appear when you're in the correct location.

To dress up the text a bit more, you can add a Live Filter.

● **Note:** You will learn more about working with text in Lesson 7.

11 In the Filters area of the Property inspector, click the Add Live Filter button, and then choose Shadow And Glow > Drop Shadow. Set the Distance to **4**, and click away from the Live Filter settings to close them.

Working with Auto Shapes

Auto Shapes, unlike other basic shapes, include additional diamond-shaped control points that let you alter visual properties, such as corner roundness. Most of these control points also have tooltips that describe how they affect the Auto Shape. You will now add an Auto Shape as a background for the watch thumbnails.

1   Choose the Chamfer Rectangle tool from the Vector section of the Tools panel (click and hold the Rectangle tool to see the other tools available).

2   Drag out the shape so it covers the width and height of the four watch thumbnails. When you release the mouse, you'll see the yellow diamonds in each corner. You'll also see that the shape takes on the properties of the last vector shape, which can make for a pretty busy looking design.

3   If necessary, change the Fill from Pattern to Solid.

4   Set the fill color to **#343434**, matching the gray background of the watches.

5   Make sure the Stroke category is set to None.

6   Click on one of the four yellow corner diamonds to toggle the corners of your shape to other designs. Keep clicking until the chamfer shape returns.

7   You can resize the total shape by clicking and dragging the fifth yellow diamond, located near the bottom right of the shape.

8   Use the Layers panel to adjust the stacking order of the new shape, so it is below the watches.

9   Reposition the shape so it is centered under the watch group. Smart Guides will help you align the objects.

10 Set the Stroke Category to Pencil > 1-Pixel Soft and the stroke color to black (#000000). Your final design should be similar to this.

▶ **Tip:** The Shapes panel (Window > Auto Shapes) contains a collection of even more complex shapes. You can download other shapes from the Adobe Exchange at www.adobe.com/cfusion/exchange/. You will have to sign up first, but membership is free.

Understanding paths and the Pen tool

The Pen tool lets you create custom shapes and paths by drawing with the mouse or a stylus. It also allows you to edit existing shapes by adding anchor points. Unlike the Pencil bitmap tool, where you basically just click and drag to draw a bitmap line, using the Pen tool involves clicking the mouse to set a straight line between two anchor points (a place where the path can change direction) or clicking and dragging to create a curved section of a path. Every time you want to change the direction of a path, you move the mouse to the desired position and then click to set an anchor point.

Let's try out the Pen tool in a new document.

1 Create a new document that is 500 x 500 pixels.

2 Set the Canvas color to white if necessary.

3 Click OK.

4 Select the Pen tool.

5 To make it easy to see the finished path, or select it later, make sure a stroke color has been applied. Black is fine.

6 Click once near the left side of the canvas.

7 Move your mouse near the middle of the canvas.

8 Click again to set another anchor point.

9 Move the mouse to the right area of the canvas.

10 This time, instead of just clicking the mouse, hold the mouse button down and *drag*. This will pull out curve control arms for that section of the path.

11 When you have drawn a curve to your satisfaction, release the mouse button. As you add more anchor points, Fireworks displays the path outline in blue.

If you move the mouse around, you will see the Pen tool is still active. To disengage the tool, do one of the following:

• Close the path (create a shape) by clicking on the original starting anchor point.

• Double-click on the last anchor point to create an open path.

Anchor point basics

Anchor points have two states: straight and curved. You can convert a straight point to a curved point by using the Pen tool to click and drag out the curve control arms, also known as Bezier control arms.

To convert a curved anchor to a straight point, just click on it once with the Pen tool. Click a second time to delete the anchor point entirely.

If you want to delete a straight anchor point, select it with the Subselection tool, and press the Delete key.

Other vector tools

Vector Path tool

The Vector Path tool can be handy if you like to draw vector shapes in a more freehand manner. While best suited for a stylus, due to the precise control and varying degrees of pressure that a tablet allows you, you can also use a mouse to draw independent paths.

Redraw Path tool

The Redraw Path tool gives you another way to edit a vector shape or path without having to use the Pen tool. Much like the Vector Path tool, you use this freehand, to draw a new path and connect it to an existing path to change its shape. Draw outside the existing path to add to the shape or draw inside to cut away from the shape. The path's stroke, fill, and effects are retained.

Freeform tool

The Freeform tool lets you bend and reshape vectors interactively instead of altering anchor points. You use this tool to push or pull any part of a path, and Fireworks adds, moves, or deletes points along the path as you change the vector object's shape.

Reshape Area tool

The Reshape Area tool is another way to distort a path. It pulls the area of all selected paths within the outer circle of the reshape-area pointer. Think of it as a smudge tool for vectors, but instead of smearing pixels, it alters a path's shape.

Path Scrubber

The Path Scrubber is an interesting tool. It doesn't change the path; rather, you use it to alter the heaviness of the stroke which is applied the path. It affects the stroke only in the areas you paint over with the tool. This can give the stroke a bit more of a hand-drawn look.

Editing paths

Creating paths and shapes is empowering (and fun!), but it's only half the battle. Knowing how to edit vectors—that is, to be able to customize them—is equally important.

Adding points with the Pen tool

You can add anchor points to an existing path using the Pen tool.

1   Make sure the path is active by selecting it with the Pointer tool.

2   Select the Pen tool.

3   Click on the path where you want the new anchor point to be; note the plus sign (+) that appears next to the Pen tool's cursor. Click once to add a straight path connection; click and drag to create a curved path section. (If you add a point to a curved segment, it is automatically a curved anchor point.)

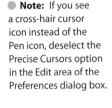

Note: If you see a cross-hair cursor icon instead of the Pen icon, deselect the Precise Cursors option in the Edit area of the Preferences dialog box.

4   To stop the Pen tool from adding to the end of an open path like this one, double-click on the last control point in the path.

Editing paths with the Subselection tool

After a path is created, you can use the Subselection tool ( ) to select and alter the location of individual anchor points, thus changing the shape of the path. The Subselection tool works similarly to the Direct Selection tool in Photoshop or Illustrator.

1   Select the Subselection tool from the Tools panel.

2   Move the tool to the middle anchor point of the path you created earlier. If the vector is no longer active (highlighted in blue), click anywhere on the path to activate it.

3   Click and drag the middle anchor point lower on the canvas. The path will redraw when you release the mouse.

Note: To use the Subselection tool on Auto Shapes or on vectors created by the Rectangle tool, you must first ungroup them (Modify > Ungroup, or Ctrl/ Command+G). They will lose their unique characteristics: Auto Shapes will lose their yellow control handles, and you will no longer be able to change the corner radius of a rectangle from within the Property inspector.

Creating custom shapes

Creating custom vector shapes opens up a lot of creative options. In this exercise, you will use the Pen tool to do this. This image has a bitmap background and a complex vector illustration of the movie's lead actor. To practice custom shapes, you'll create a stylized background to run behind the movie title in this design. First you will import the movie title.

Importing and resizing a vector object

1 Open street_scene.png.

2 Choose File > Import, and browse to the Lesson04 folder.

3 Locate and select the movie_title.png file, and click OK to return to the canvas. The import tool icon replaces the standard cursor.

4 Click anywhere on the canvas to import the title at its original size.

5 Resize the title to a specific size by choosing Modify > Transform > Numeric Transform.

6 Change the sizing option from Scale to Resize.

7 Set the width to **467** pixels. The height will adjust automatically—so long as Constrain Proportions is selected—giving you dimensions of 467 x 342.

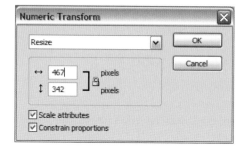

● **Note:** Did you notice that the movie title's overall quality did not change after resizing? That's because the title is made up of a group of vectors. And, to ensure that the text style does not change from designer to designer, the text was converted from true text to paths.

8 Click OK.

9 Use the Pointer tool to position the title so the letter "Y" is near the brim of the detective's hat. The x and y coordinates should be around 198 x 121.

Drawing the shape

Now you're ready to draw the shape for the title. You will do your best to imitate the shape shown in the following figure. It's made up of a series of straight anchor point segments. This is a custom shape, so don't worry if you don't create an exact match. To help you further, you can make the original shape visible in the Layers panel and use it as a guide.

1   Lock all other objects in the Layers panel (click on the empty square to the left of each object name) so you don't accidentally move or edit them, and hide the detective so you can see the full vector example.

2   Select the Pen tool.

3   In the Property inspector, set the Fill to None and the stroke Basic > Hard Line. Set the stroke's color to #990000 and the Texture to 0%.

4   Click and release the mouse to set each point for the shape. There is no need to click and drag any of these points as you set them, because they all need to be straight lines.

5   When you bring the cursor back to your starting point, you will notice the icon changes to the Pen tool icon with a small circle, indicating you can close the path by clicking. This closed path is your custom shape.

6   If you were using the original image as a guide, hide it now in the Layers panel.

7   Reselect the new vector object you just created in the Layers panel.

8   Select the Subselection tool.

9   If necessary, you can reposition any anchor points in the new object; use the mouse to reposition anchor points. Note how both paths extending from the anchor point adjust based on the new location of the anchor point. Feel free to adjust anchor points until you have the shape you want.

10 Save the file.

Customizing fills and strokes

Creating a custom shape is just the beginning; once you have a vector object on the canvas, you can apply a variety of fill and stroke effects to it as well. Here, you're going to customize the look of your newly created custom shape by adding a gradient and a stylized stroke effect.

Adding a gradient fill

1   If necessary, select the custom object you just created.

2   Choose Gradient > Linear from the Fill Category menu in the Property inspector. A standard linear gradient appears.

3   Select the Pointer tool. A black control arm appears.

This "arm" controls the location, direction, angle, and length of the gradient fill. The arm has a circle control point at one end and a square control point at the other. The circle controls the position/starting point for the gradient; the square controls the angle and length. By default, the linear gradient runs from top to bottom, the full height of the object.

4   Use the mouse to click and drag the circle point so it rests on the top edge of the shape. As you drag, the gradient updates live on the canvas.

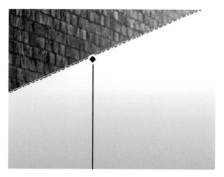

5   Move the mouse onto the arm itself. A rotation icon appears. Click and drag the arm so that is roughly parallel to the angle of the shape.

6   Drag the circle point again so it is positioned in the gap of the shape at the lower left.

7 Drag the square control point to shorten the gradient and to change its angle.

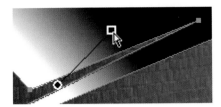

8 Click the Fill Color box. This will open the Edit Gradient pop-up window.

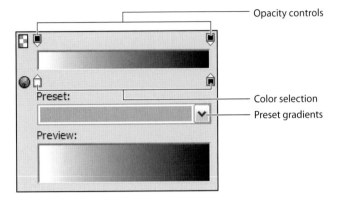

Opacity controls

Color selection

Preset gradients

9 Click the left color swatch and when the color picker appears, type **#252A41** in the input field. Then press Enter or Return.

10 Click the right color swatch, input **#C3112E**, and press Enter or Return.

11 Still within the Property inspector, click the Add Live Filters button, and choose Shadow And Glow > Drop Shadow to add a drop shadow to the object.

Customizing the stroke

Much like adding a fill to a vector, styling the stroke can also add impact and interest to an object. The plain red stroke we've got currently is OK, but to really give a sense of grittiness and danger, you will customize the stroke using one of the preset Stroke categories.

1 Making sure the object is still selected, set the Tip Size to **38**.

2 Set the Stroke category to Oil > Splatter.

3 Choose the Stroke category menu again, and choose Stroke Options.

4 Select the Fill Over Stroke option, and click away from the Stroke Options panel to close it.

5 Change the stroke's Edge softness to **19**.

6 Choose DNA from the Texture menu, and set the value to **30%**.

7 In the Layers panel, unlock the layers, unhide the detective layer, and position the shape you created below it in the stacking order. This puts both the detective and the imported text object in front and makes them fully visible.

8 Save the file.

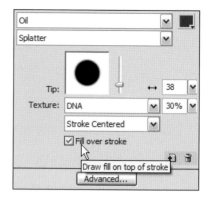

▶ **Tip:** Dragging layers up and down in the Layers panel moves them away or toward the canvas, respectively. You can also choose one of the four options in the Modify > Arrange menu to alter the stacking order of selected objects: Bring to Front, Bring Forward, Send Backward, and Send To Back. If you use this feature frequently, memorizing the keyboard shortcuts will be a great time-saver.

Applying a pattern to a vector object

Adding a pattern works much the same way as adding a gradient. The available preset patterns are arranged alphabetically in Fill Category Pattern submenu in the Property the selection list (or you can create your own). They are bitmap images that have been designed to seamlessly tile inside a vector shape.

1 Create an exact copy of the custom shape by choosing Edit > Clone.

2 Choose Pattern > Wood from the Fill Category menu in the Property inspector.

As with the gradient, you will here see the control arms that allow you to change the direction of the pattern or even distort it.

3 Place the cursor over one of the arms (not the points) to rotate the pattern to suit the orientation of your object.

4 Delete the object from the Layers panel.

▶ **Tip:** The Path panel (Window > Others > Path) opens up a lot of possibilities for creative design, even if you are not a whiz with the Pen tool. You can punch out corners, knock holes out of a shape, distort existing paths, and have a great degree of control over anchor points.

Review questions

1 What is one of the main differences between bitmaps and vectors when scaling is applied?

2 When drawing a rectangle, how can you easily round the corners of the shape?

3 What are Auto Shapes, and where can you find them?

4 How do you edit the control points of a vector object once it has been drawn?

5 What is the Pen tool used for?

Review answers

1 Vector images do not degrade in quality when they are resized, either smaller or larger, and bitmap images do.

2 Before releasing the mouse, press the Up Arrow key to increase the roundness of the rectangle's corners. Press the Down Arrow key to reduce the corner radius.

3 Auto Shapes are objects that include additional diamond-shaped control points that let you alter visual properties, such as corner roundness. Dragging a control point alters the associated visual property. Most control points have tooltips that describe how they affect the Auto Shape, too. Basic Auto Shape drawing tools are found in the Tools panel; more complex ones are found in the Shapes panel.

4 To edit the control points of an existing vector object, select the Subselection tool, click on a control point, and drag the control point to reposition the paths connected to it.

5 The Pen tool lets you create custom shapes and paths by drawing with the mouse or a stylus. It also allows you to add anchor points to existing paths. Using the Pen tool involves clicking the mouse to set a straight line between two anchor points (a place where the path can change direction) or clicking and dragging to create a curved section of a path. Every time you want to change the direction of a path, you move the mouse to the desired position and then click to set another anchor point.

5 THE LAYERS PANEL— YOUR BEST FRIEND

Lesson overview

Layers are probably the most important workflow and design tool you have in Fireworks. Simply put, they add structure to your document. In previous lessons, you manipulated layers as directed, but in this lesson you will more fully explore the use of layers in a design.

In this lesson, you'll learn how to do the following:

- Create new layers

- Create sub layers

- Change the stacking order of layers

- Rename layers

- Protect layers and objects

- Access layer options

 This lesson will take about 40 minutes to complete. Copy the Lesson05 folder into the Lessons folder that you created on your hard drive for these projects (or create it now), if you haven't already done so. As you work on this lesson, you won't preserve the start files. If you need to restore the start files, copy them from the *Adobe Fireworks CS4 Classroom in a Book* CD.

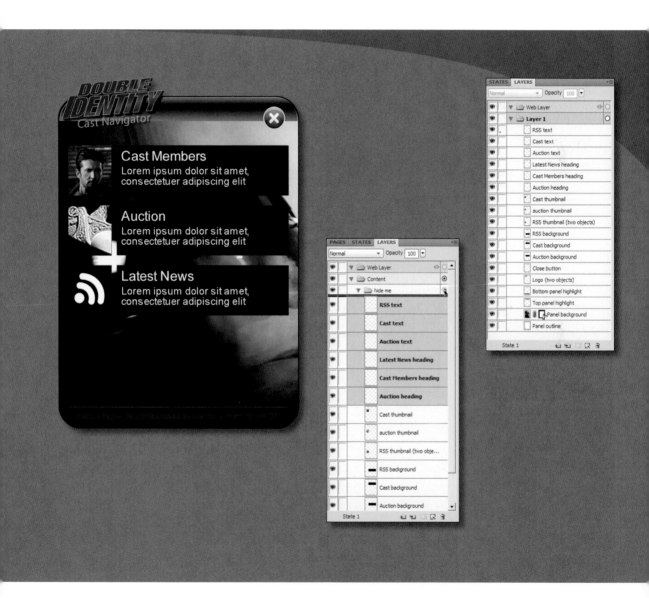

Layers are probably the most important workflow and design tool you have in Fireworks. Simply put, they add structure to your document.

About layers

You can place multiple images or text objects in a single layer, and with a simple design, this may be fine. But as you add more objects to a design, keeping everything in a single layer becomes problematic; it gets harder to locate specific images or text areas because you have to scroll through a very long list.

Layers allow objects to be independent from each other. Used properly, they impose a sense of order in your document. You can add or remove layers, or the objects within them, without affecting other elements in the design. You can change how objects within layers interact with other layers by changing the stacking order of layers. As you change the order of layers, objects overlap differently.

You can hide layers from view, to make it easier to select or work with other objects, and you can lock layers so they will not be selected accidentally. You can even share layers across specific states in a design, or specific pages in a design.

Every document opened in Fireworks—even an untouched, empty document—contains a Web layer. The Web layer is where interactive objects such as slices and hotspots are stored. Regardless of your plans for the file, the Web layer cannot be deleted. If the file is new, or has never been opened in Fireworks before (for example, a new digital photo), by default it will also include a generic layer called Layer 1.

Getting started with layers

1   If you haven't already done so, copy the Lesson05 folder to your hard drive.

2   In Fireworks, choose File > New.

3   Set the Canvas Size to 500 x 500 pixels, and the Canvas Color to white.

4   Click OK.

5   Select the Rectangle tool from the Vector section of the Tools panel.

6   Draw a rectangle on the canvas. In the Layers panel, notice that the shape is automatically added to Layer 1 as a unique object. Everything you add to a Fireworks document is added as a separate object. You can see the new object here, conveniently named Rectangle by default.

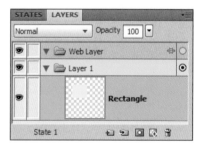

7   Close the file without saving it.

Identifying objects

Fireworks highlights independent objects as you move the mouse over them. As your mouse glides over objects on the canvas, you will see different areas highlight in red. This highlight indicates the independent object in that particular spot; you can then click to select that specific object. In this and the following sections, you'll examine the cast_navigator_start. png file to see layers at work.

1   Choose File > Open.

2   Browse to the Lesson05 folder.

3   Select the cast_navigator_start.png file, and click Open.

4   Select the Pointer tool if it is not already active.

5   Move your mouse around the canvas area, and note how different areas highlight in red.

Naming objects

A good habit to get into is giving your objects meaningful names.

1   In order to see more of the Layers panel, and to minimize the need for scrolling, collapse the other visible panel groups by clicking once on the gray tab bar next to the panel names in other (non-Layers) panel groups.

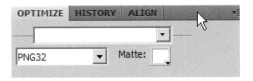

● **Note:** In the rush to create a file, you may overlook this essential part of structuring your document. But if you have to pass the file onto a co-worker, a document full of unnamed objects can be very hard to navigate and make sense of.

2   Select the photo of the actor on the canvas.

3   In the Layers panel, double-click on the highlighted object called—none too descriptively—Bitmap.

4   Change it to **Cast thumbnail**.

5   Click on the second thumbnail image on the canvas, and rename it
    Auction thumbnail.

6   Click on the third thumbnail image on the canvas, the group, and rename it
    RSS thumbnail (2 objects).

    The two objects you just renamed will now be located near the top of the
    Layers panel.

7   Proceed to rename the other objects, in this order, from the top down, as follows:

    • RSS text

    • Cast text

    • Auction text

    • Latest News heading

    • Cast Members heading

    • Auction heading

    • RSS background

    • Cast background

    • Auction background

    • Close button

    • Logo (two objects)

    • Bottom panel highlight

    • Top panel highlight

    • Panel background

    • Panel outline

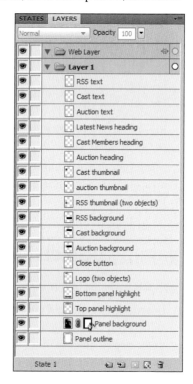

Rearranging objects within a layer

By completing the previous exercise, it should be pretty obvious that objects are,
well, all over the place in this design! Let's add some structure first by rearranging
some of the objects.

1   Locate the Cast thumbnail object in the Layers panel.

2   Drag it upward to the top of Layer 1 in the panel.

●**Note:** Dragging an object to the top of a layer can be tricky; if you can't seem to place it at the
top, it will most likely drop in as the second from the top image. At that point, simply drag the RSS
thumbnail object below the Cast thumbnail object.

3   Save the file.

Adding and naming layers

Things are a little more organized now. To help structure the file even more, you will add a new layer and some sub layers to Layers panel.

1   Create a new layer by clicking the New/Duplicate Layer button at the bottom of the Layers panel. This layer, appropriately called Layer 2, will appear above the existing layer.

2   Double-click the new Layer 2 in the Layers panel, and change its name to **Content**.

3   Double-click on the original Layer 1, and rename it **Interface**.

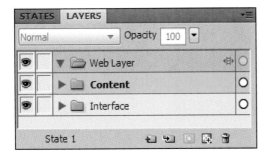

Moving objects from one layer to another

Now that you have a Content layer, you can fill it with—you guessed it—content.

1 In the Interface layer, click the Cast thumbnail object.

2 Scroll down until you see the Auction background object.

3 Hold down the Shift key, and select this object. All objects from Cast thumbnail to Auction background are now selected.

● **Note:** You can also cut selected objects, select a new layer, and paste the objects, or you can click and drag an object (or a series of selected objects) to a different layer.

4 Drag the selected objects into the Content layer. The easiest way to do this is to drag the radio button from the Interface layer onto the radio button on the Content layer.

Now all the content is in its own layer, and the interface items are in their own layer as well.

Creating sub layers

For additional structure, you can use sub layers to contain related content within a single layer.

1 Make sure the Content layer is selected.

2 Click the New Sub Layer button to add a sub layer in the Content layer.

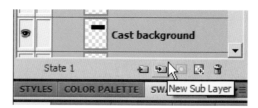

3 Rename this new sub layer **Hide Me**.

4 Shift-click to select the RSS text to Auction heading objects.

5 Drag the radio button from the Content layer onto the radio button on the Hide Me layer to move these six text objects.

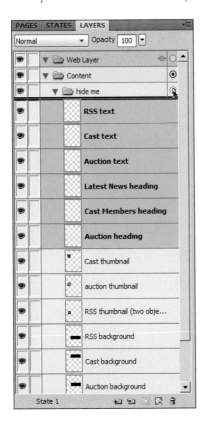

6 Click the Expand/Collapse Layer icon to collapse the Hide Me sub layer. If the text objects disappear from view in the panel, you know they are in the right place.

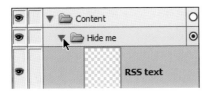

Note: Often you will place text content into a design for placement/layout purposes only. The Fireworks text is not expected to be used beyond this design stage. By placing this content into a layer of its own, you can quickly hide the content from view. By naming the layer Hide Me, it's made pretty obvious that this content is only temporary.

With these few simple steps, your file is more organized. You can easily expand or collapse the individual layers in the Layers panel to display only the objects you need to work on.

7 Click the Expand/Collapse Layer icons to minimize the Content and Interface layers. You can see how much more manageable this design has become.

Protecting layers

When a layer is locked, no object within it can be selected or deleted by accident.

1 Click in the Lock column for the Interface layer.

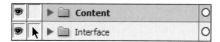

2 Expand the Interface layer. Notice the ghost of a lock appears beside each object.

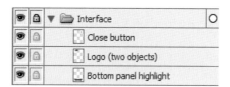

3 Try to select one of the objects in the Interface layer. You can't, because they are all locked.

If your concern is only to protect certain objects rather than the entire layer, you can do that, too:

4 Right-click (Windows) or Control-click (Mac) on the layer in the Layers panel.

5 Choose Unlock All from the context menu.

6 Lock the layers named Bottom panel highlight, Top panel highlight, Panel background, and Panel outline.

7 Move the mouse to the canvas, and hover over the logo and the Close button. Red highlights indicate those objects are selectable.

8 Hover over the bottom of the panel. No red indicators appear. These objects are locked.

9 Unlock the objects individually by selecting the lock icon beside each object name.

10 Save the file.

Layer options

Like many panels in Fireworks, the Layers panel has options for configuring the panel, adding new layers or sub layers, and determining how a layer interacts with other pages or states within a Fireworks design.

Access the Layers panel's options by right-clicking (or Control-clicking) any layer or by opening the Layers panel menu in the top right corner of the panel (▼≡).

Among other options, you can increase the size of your the thumbnails by selecting Thumbnail Options. This will make the images easier to recognize.

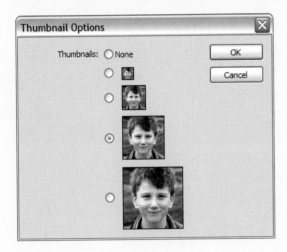

Review questions

1 What is the importance of layers?

2 What special layer does every Fireworks document have?

3 How do you change the stacking order of a layer or object, and why would you do this?

4 How do you move objects from one layer to another?

5 How do you access layer options?

Review answers

1 Layers add structure to your document.

   As you add more objects to a design, keeping everything in a single layer gets problematic; it gets harder to locate specific images or text areas because you have to scroll through a very long list. With objects sorted into multiple layers, you can quickly collapse layers to see your main design structure or expand a specific layer to select an individual object.

   Layers allow objects to be independent from each other. You can add or remove layers or the objects within them without affecting other elements in the design. You can change how objects within layers interact with other layers by changing the stacking order of layers.

2 Every Fireworks document has a Web layer. This is where interactive elements called hotspots and slices are stored. The Web layer does not have to be used in a design, but it cannot be deleted.

3 You change the stacking order of a layer by dragging it above or below an existing layer. You would do this to change how objects in the layer overlap or blend with the other layers.

4 You can move objects in one of several ways within the Layers panel:

   • Cut and paste a selected object from one layer to another.

   • Drag a selected object or objects from layer to layer.

   • Select an object or objects within one layer, and drag the associated radio button from the original layer to the radio button on the target layer.

5 You can right-click (or Control-click) any layer to invoke the layer options context menu, or you can open the Layers panel menu at the top-right corner of the Layers panel.

6 MASKING

Lesson overview

Masking opens up a world of creative options, and adds flexibility to your designs as well, because with masks you are not permanently deleting pixels; you're merely hiding them from view. Combined with using gradient fills, you can get some very customized results. Fireworks lets you work with both bitmap and vector masks easily and seamlessly. In this lesson, you'll learn how to do the following:

- Create a bitmap mask from a selection

- Edit a bitmap mask using the Brush tool

- Create a vector mask from a custom vector shape

- Edit the vector mask and change its properties using the Property inspector

- Use the Auto Vector Mask command

 This lesson will take about 90 minutes to complete. Copy the Lesson06 folder into the Lessons folder that you created on your hard drive for these projects (or create it now), if you haven't already done so. As you work on this lesson, you won't preserve the start files. If you need to restore the start files, copy them from the *Adobe Fireworks CS4 Classroom in a Book* CD.

Masking opens up a world of creative options, adding flexibility to your designs as well, because you are not permanently deleting pixels; you're merely hiding them from view.

About masks

In this lesson, you will work with masks in the process of creating a banner ad for the promotion of the Double Identity movie, and you'll have a chance to brush up on importing images and using the Pen and Subselection tools along the way.

Before we get into that, we'll give a basic definition, talk about the differences between the two types of masking, and take a look at the finished artwork to give you an idea of where you're going.

Open up the movie_banner_final.png file from the Lesson06 folder. In this file, masks have been used on the cars and the actors. In many cases, the mask fill has been changed to a gradient, to provide a more realistic fade into the background.

In a nutshell, masks hide or show parts of an object or image. Masks are a non-destructive way of cropping objects in your design, without permanently deleting anything. A mask can be edited or discarded at any time. You can also permanently apply a mask, flattening it to the image being masked. There are two basic kinds of mask: bitmap and vector.

Bitmap masks

Bitmap masks hide bitmap image data using a pixel-based mask.

You can create bitmap masks using selections or using the Brush ( ) tool.

Use any of the bitmap selection tools to create your selection. Decide on the type of edge you want for the selection (Hard, Anti-alias, Feather) using the Live Marquee settings in the Property inspector. Then just draw your selection. Bitmap selections can create masks only for other bitmaps.

Using the Brush tool, you can easily create or edit the mask live on the canvas, just by painting. If you set your brush color to a shade of gray, the pixels painted over will be semitransparent. Black hides, white reveals, and shades of gray produce semi-transparency. (We'll remind you of this important basic concept later in the lesson.)

You can also mask one bitmap image with another. The darker tones in a photo used as a mask will hide areas on the image being masked. Lighter tones will reveal parts of the masked image.

Original image

Beginning to paint a bitmap selection with the Brush tool

The final masked image

Vector masks

Vector masking is one of the most powerful features in Fireworks. Like bitmap masks, vector masks are a nondestructive way of cropping a bitmap image, where both the bitmap and vector remain editable after the mask has been applied. You can also mask another vector shape with a vector mask.

Compared to bitmap masks, vector masks tend to have a higher degree of control and accuracy, because you use a path, not a brush, to create them. It's easy to change the fill or stroke of a vector mask. Generating the same type of effect with a bitmap mask can be more time-consuming.

Vector masks use one of two modes: Path Outline or Grayscale Appearance. You can change the mode in the Property inspector.

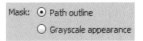

In Path Outline mode, the vector mask acts like a cookie cutter, using the shape of the path to act as the mask.

In Grayscale Appearance, any bitmap information in the vector's fill gets converted to a grayscale alpha channel. Grayscale Appearance uses the pixel values of the vector's fill *and* the vector shape itself to create the mask. So if your vector mask has a range of tones in it—such as a gradient fill—the image will be hidden or revealed based on those tones. Just like with bitmap masks, black hides, white reveals, and shades of gray produce semitransparency, as in this example, where a linear gradient has been used to fill the vector shape.

The convenient Auto Vector Mask feature works in this way as well. We'll try that out later in the chapter.

Whether you have drawn a vector shape using a tool from the Tools panel or have used the Pen tool to create your own custom shape, you can easily apply it as a mask.

Designing the banner ad

The banner you are going to work with in this lesson has many elements to it—imported assets, masks, gradients, text, layers, and so on. You will begin by creating the new, basic document to hold all your further work.

Creating the document

1   Choose File > New.

2   In the New Document dialog box, set the dimensions to **730** pixels wide by **90** pixels high.

3   Click on the color swatch to set a custom Canvas color.

4 Choose black (#000000) from the Color Picker.

5 Click OK.

Ultimately, this document will use multiple layers. You will add those now.

6 Double-click the existing Layer 1 name in the Layers panel, and rename it **background**.

7 Click the New/Duplicate Layer icon (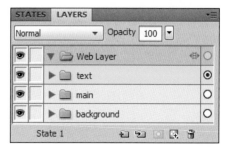) at the bottom of the Layers panel.

8 Name the new layer **main**.

9 Repeat step 7 to create one more layer, and name it **text**.

Adding the background

The background for the final banner is not just a flat color; it's got some depth, and variation in tone. You will create that now.

1 Lock the text and main layers by clicking the empty box beside the layer names. This will force any new objects into the background layer.

2 Select the Rectangle tool, and draw a rectangle the same size as the canvas (730 x 90 pixels).

3 In the Property inspector, change the Fill Category to Gradient > Starburst.

4 Click the Fill color box to open the Edit Gradient pop-up window.

Editing gradient colors

Now you will set the colors for the gradient.

1 Click on the far-left color swatch.

2 Use the Eyedropper tool to select the black color swatch.

Click color swatch to launch Color Picker

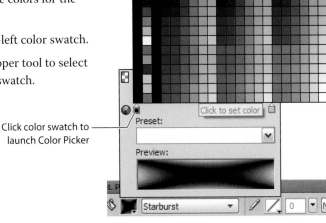

3 Add the next color by clicking just below the gradient ramp, where your cursor becomes an arrow with a plus sign next to it. A new gradient color swatch appears.

4 Click the color swatch, and change the existing color value in the input field to #**535973**.

5 Press Enter or Return.

6 Continue adding color swatches to the gradient by typing the following values into the field: **181C25**, **000000**, **716F64**, and **626784**.

7 Place the color swatches so that they resemble this figure, and click away from the Edit Gradient pop-up window when you're finished.

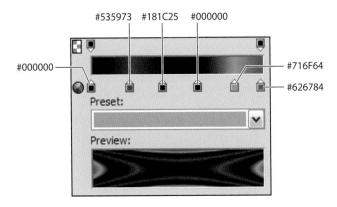

Editing gradient direction and angle

You can alter the angle and direction of a gradient by moving the gradient control arm (or arms).

With the rectangle still active, and the gradient applied, you should see two control arms. The arms are normally black, so we've outlined them in white here to make them easier to see.

Controls origin/position of gradient

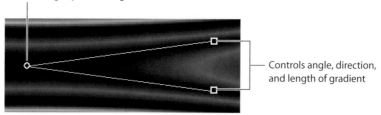

Controls angle, direction, and length of gradient

1 Choose the Pointer tool from the Tools panel.

2 Change the length and angle of the upper gradient arm by dragging the square control point until it is similar to what you see below. Again, we have outlined the control arms in white so it's easier for you to see the change.

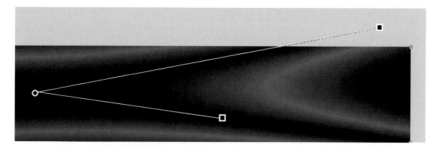

3 Lock the background layer.

4 Save your file as **movie_banner_working.png**.

Importing assets

1 Unlock the text layer by clicking on the lock icon beside the layer name.

2 Choose File > Import.

3 Locate and open the movie_title.png file in the Lesson06 folder.

4 When the import icon () appears, position the cursor near the left side of the canvas. Click and drag until the width is approximately 160 and the height 78 pixels. Tooltips do not appear when you are scaling an imported image, so keep an eye on the Property inspector.

5 Release the mouse. The text appears.

6 In the Property inspector, set the *x* and *y* coordinates for the title to **30** and **2** pixels respectively.

7 In the Layers panel, rename the object **movie title**.

8 Lock the text layer, and unlock the main layer.

9 Choose File > Import again, and open the policecar1.png file.

10 Drag the import icon until the width is approximately 80 pixels, and release the mouse.

11 In the Property inspector, set the *x* and *y* coordinates to **157** and **44** pixels respectively.

● **Note:** This text is actually a series of paths that have been grouped together.

12 In the Layers panel, rename the object **car1**.

13 Import the policecar2.png file.

14 Release the mouse when the width reaches approximately 56 pixels. Set its *x* and *y* coordinates to **217** and **24** pixels respectively.

15 In the Layers panel, rename the object **car2**.

Using the Auto Vector Mask for quick fades

You'll do more complicated masking shortly, but for these police cars, the Auto Vector Mask is just the feature to use. This command can be used on vector or bitmap objects.

1 Select car1 in the Layers panel.

2 Choose Commands > Creative > Auto Vector Mask. A dialog box appears.

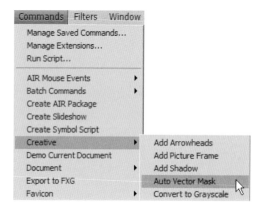

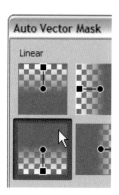

3 Choose the vertical linear gradient, solid to transparent.

4 Move the dialog box so it is not covering the car, and you will see the effect previewed on the canvas.

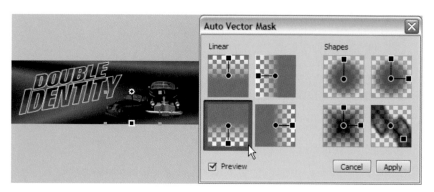

5 Click the Apply button.

6 Use the Pointer tool to reposition the gradient so it begins lower on the car. Place the circle control handle on the hood.

7 Drag the square control handle up and slightly to the right, to shorten the gradient and change the angle. The bottom front wheel of the car should appear to fade into the background.

8 Select car2 from the Layers panel, or use the Pointer tool to select it on the canvas.

9 Choose Commands > Creative > Auto Vector Mask again.

10 Choose the Radial shape gradient, and click Apply.

11 Use the Pointer tool to reposition the gradient circle control handle on the right side of the hood.

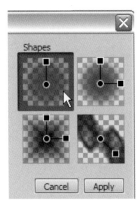

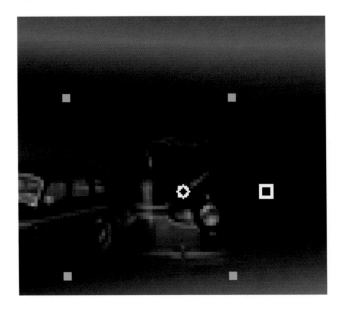

12 Drag the square control handle to the lower right. This will fade the top and left sides of the car, blending it with the other car and the background.

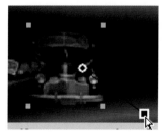

13 Save the file.

▶ **Tip:** Thanks to the Live Preview of the Auto Vector Mask effects, not only can you see the result of your choice before you apply it, the Property inspector will also show you what type of gradient is being used to create the effect.

Importing Photoshop images

You are getting *lots* of practice importing images. You will import two more images now, but there's a twist. These images are Photoshop (PSD) files. Fireworks has some special features when importing such files, even if the file is only a simple, single image.

1 Choose File > Import, and browse to the Lesson06 folder.

2 Open the mark_actor06.psd file. The Photoshop File Import Options dialog box appears. There are many settings here, but you are only concerned about image size at this time.

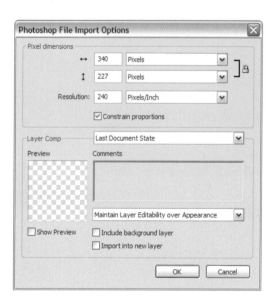

3 Set the width to **340** pixels. The height will adjust automatically.

4 Click OK.

5 When the import icon appears, just click on the canvas once to load the image at the previously set dimensions.

6 Reposition the image to X: 97, Y: -45 pixels.

7 Rename the image in the Layers panel to **Mark**.

8 Lock and hide the Mark object.

9 Choose File > Import again.

10 Open the wendy.psd file.

11 Set the width to **290** pixels, and click OK.

12 When the import icon appears, click on the canvas once to load the image at the previously set dimensions.

13 Rename the object in the Layers panel to **Wendy**.

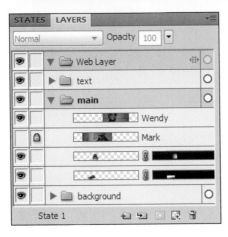

Creating and editing masks

You've now come quite a long way with the banner ad file, and a lot of the assets are in place—enough to notice that there is far too much background visible in both of the actor photos. You will use masks to hide most of it.

Creating a vector mask

Comparing the completed version with your working version, you can see that Wendy is facing the opposite direction from Mark. You will alter your image of Wendy so it (or she) faces the same way.

1 Select the Wendy image.

2 Right-click (Windows) or Control-click (Mac) on Wendy's face on the canvas. A context menu appears.

3 Choose Transform > Flip Horizontal.

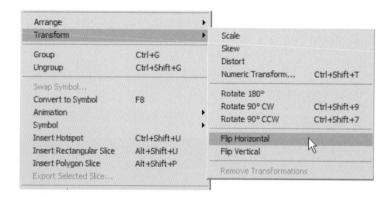

4 Set the position to X: 340, Y: -39.

5 Select the Ellipse tool from the Tools panel.

6 Change the edge from Anti-alias to Feather, with a value of 10, if necessary.

7 Draw an oval shape around Wendy's face.

8 Release the mouse. The vector ellipse will appear, filled with the last Fill Category option used for a vector. The category needs to be a gradient ellipse; if this is not what shows up in the Fill Category field, choose Gradient > Ellipse from the Fill Category menu.

9 Change the gradient in the Fill Color box to the White, Black preset.

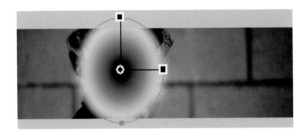

10 With the vector shape still selected, choose Edit > Cut.

11 Use the Pointer tool to select the Wendy photo.

12 Choose Edit > Paste As Mask.

13 The ellipse now masks the photo of Wendy, using the Path Outline mode.

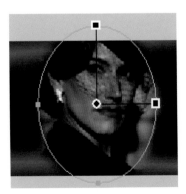

Changing vector mask attributes

As you learned earlier, Path Outline mode works like a cookie cutter. For the Wendy image, though, we want a subtle vignette, fading the background around her face. To do this, you must switch to Grayscale Appearance mode.

1 Select the Grayscale Appearance option (radio button) in the Property inspector. The photo fades at the edges of the vector shape.

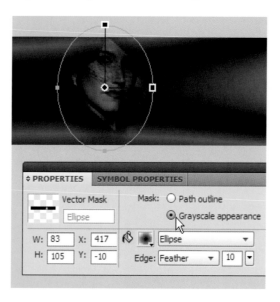

2 Change the Fill Color to the White, Black preset if the fill color has changed.

3 Move the circle control point of the gradient so that it is near her nose. You will find this easier to do if you zoom in to at least 200%.

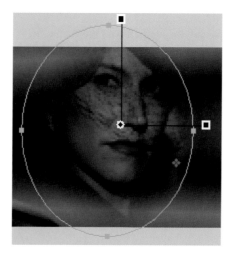

4 Use the Pointer tool to set the arms to a clock position of roughly 4:35.

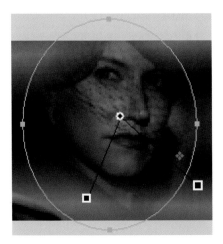

5 Extend the left arm slightly out of the canvas area.

6 Hide and lock the Wendy object.

▶ **Tip:** Once a mask has been added, you can reposition the image being masked by dragging the small blue control icon (⊞) in the middle of the image. This is visible when the image object, rather than the mask, is active.

Editing a vector mask

When a vector mask is made active from the Layers panel, you can use the Property inspector to change the Fill Category and Edge settings, as well as those of the stroke (category, size, and edge).

You edit the vector shape itself by choosing the Subselection tool and repositioning the vector control points, just as you would with a regular vector shape. You can even add points by using the Pen tool. For more information on editing vectors, make sure to read Lesson 4.

Converting a bitmap selection to a mask

Sometimes cropping and masking go hand in hand. If you have a small area that you want to mask within a larger image, it may be a good idea to first crop out the unnecessary parts of the larger image. For the Mark image, you won't need the surrounding background at all, so you will crop the image first, and then make a selection mask.

1   Unlock and reveal the Mark object in the Layers panel.

2   Choose Edit > Crop Selected Bitmap.

3   Adjust the cropping marquee so that you exclude the background on either side of the detective.

4   Press Enter or Return to crop the image.

5   Reposition the image to approximately X: 215, Y: -45. The exact position will vary depending on how much you cropped the image.

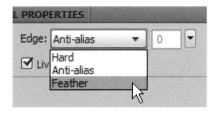

● **Note:** To refresh your memory on how to use the Lasso tools, you may want to review Lesson 3 before proceeding.

6   Select the Polygon Lasso tool.

7   Make sure the Lasso edge is set to Feather, with a value of **5**. The Live Marquee can remain selected.

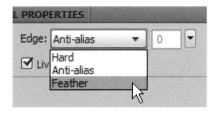

8   Trace a selection around the detective. Don't be concerned if the selection is not 100% accurate; you will remedy this in the next exercise.

9   Click the Add Mask button (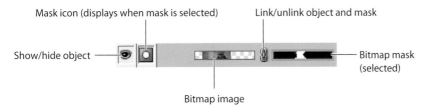) at the bottom of the Layers panel. The background disappears from the Mark object.

Editing a bitmap mask

Notice that the mask object has a green highlight around it in the Layers panel. You will also see the mask icon appear beside the object name.

Mask icon (displays when mask is selected)   Link/unlink object and mask

Show/hide object ————   ———— Bitmap mask
                                                                                          (selected)

Bitmap image

This indicates that the mask—and not the image—is active. It is important the mask remain active while you are performing these next steps. If at any time the mask is deselected, just click on it in the Layers panel.

Take a look at the mask. The color black has replaced the non-selected area. Remember that the color black, when painted on a bitmap mask object, hides pixels. White, on the other hand, reveals pixels.

1   Zoom in to 200%.

2   Select the Brush tool.

3   Press the D key to set the brush color to black (the default color).

4   Make sure the Stroke Category is set to Soft Rounded (if necessary, choose Basic > Soft Rounded from the Stroke Category pop-up menu).

5 Change the Tip Size value to 10 pixels, the Edge Softness to 100 pixels. The Texture amount should be 0%.

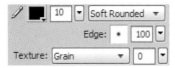

6 Paint over any areas of the background that were missed when you drew the original bitmap selection with the Polygon Lasso tool.

7 Press the X key to switch the brush color to white.

8 Find an area on the actor that was masked by accident. Paint over the area. The mistakenly hidden pixels are revealed.

If you end up revealing areas you don't want, switch back to black and paint over those areas.

⬤ **Note:** If you didn't make any mistakes while creating the selection, you can still test this out by painting over part of the background. The area under the brush reappears when you paint with white, and disappears when you paint with black.

Changing colors quickly

When working with bitmap masks, you may want to switch from black to white to gray to customize the mask. You can do this quickly with these shortcuts:

• Press the B key to switch to the Brush tool.

• Press the D key to set the color boxes to their default colors (black for stroke, white for fill).

• Press the X key to toggle the current colors between stroke and fill.

Applying Live Filters to a masked image

To give the two actors a darker, grittier, and mysterious look, you will apply a Live Filter to each of them. You'll recall that the advantage to Live Filters is that they remain editable at all times.

1 Reveal and unlock the layer called Wendy.

2 In the Layers panel, drag the Wendy layer underneath the Mark layer. Mark is large in the design, so it makes more visual sense to have him in the foreground, in case of any overlap between the two actor images.

3 Hold down the Shift key, and use the Pointer tool to select both actors.

4 Click the Add Live Filters (+) button in the Filters category of the Property inspector, and choose Adjust Color > Brightness/Contrast.

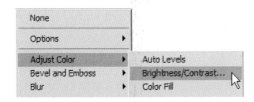

5 Set the Brightness to **-20** and the Contrast to **20**, and then click OK. Because both images were selected, the effect is applied simultaneously to both.

6 If the settings are not to your liking, select one of the objects, and then click the *i* icon beside the Live Filter name in the Property inspector. The dialog box will open again, and you can edit the settings.

Adding the silhouette

Your last graphical touch will be adding in the silhouette of a man. You have two options for this last image. You can follow the "Extra credit" steps, in which you begin with the regular image and create the bitmap selection and convert it to a vector shape, or you can continue here with step 1 in the main exercise and simply import the cameo.png file.

1 Choose File > Import.

2 Open cameo.png.

3 When the Import icon appears, click on the canvas to load the image at its original size.

4 In the Property inspector, set the *x* and *y* coordinates to 611 and -1 pixels respectively.

5 Save the file.

Extra credit: Create a vector silhouette

If you want to dig a little deeper into the project, here are the steps we used to create the silhouette vector shape from a bitmap image.

1 Choose File > Open, and browse for ManInAHat.png.

2 Select the Polygon Lasso tool.

3 Set the edge to Anti-alias. The Live Marquee can remain selected.

4 Trace around the outline of the man in the hat. You will need to add a top to the hat, as that was cropped in the original photo.

When you get back to the starting point, the lasso icon will change ($\boxtimes$), indicating you can close the selection.

5 Choose Select > Convert Marquee To Path. The selection is removed, and a new vector object takes its place.

6   Make sure the Fill Category is set to Solid and the Fill Color to Black.

7   If you need to adjust the silhouette, use the Pen tool to add extra control points, or click and drag on existing points to convert the path to a curved segment. To adjust the points themselves, use the Subselection tool. When you are satisfied with the overall silhouette, save the file.

8   Copy the silhouette (Edit > Copy).

9   Switch to the movie_banner_working.png file, and choose Edit > Paste.

You see that the shape is too large, and facing the wrong direction.

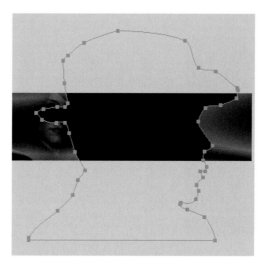

10   Right-click (or Control-click) on the shape, and choose Transform > Flip Horizontal.

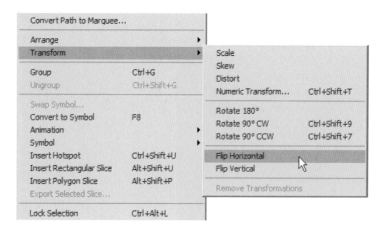

11   Select the Scale tool.

12 Hold down the Shift key (to constrain proportions), and drag in from a corner to reduce the size of the silhouette to about 100 x 96 pixels. These values may differ slightly, depending on the shape of the silhouette. Move the cursor inside the object to reposition it.

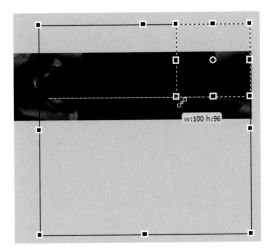

13 Move the cursor just outside the scale handles. You will see a rotate icon appear.

14 Click and drag counterclockwise to angle the face downward.

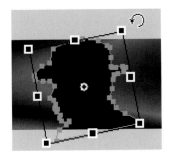

15 Press Enter or Return to commit to the changes.

16 In the Property inspector, set the *x* and *y* coordinates to approximately 611 and -1 pixels respectively.

17 Choose File > Save.

Final touches

There are several finishing touches you have to add to this design: you'll put in some more text, tweak the position of some objects, and add an accent highlight behind the movie title.

Adding text

First you will add the promotional text.

1 Lock the main layer, and unlock the text layer.

2 Select the Text tool.

3 Choose Arial Black from the Font Family menu, font size 12 points, in the Property inspector. If you don't have Arial Black, select a similarly bold font.

4 Leave the text color black—or you can temporarily change it to white so it is easier to see. You will be doing more with the text later on, so the color is not very important at this time.

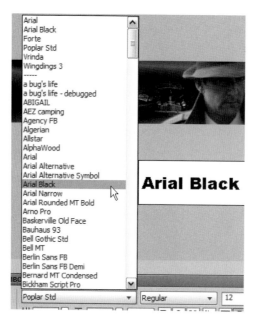

5 Move the cursor to the canvas just below the movie title.

6 Type **COMING SUMMER 2009.**

7 Highlight "2009."

8 Choose Forte from the Font Family menu. If you don't have Forte, choose a bold, sketch-like font, such as Brush Script.

9 Highlight "COMING SUMMER."

10 Set the Horizontal Scale to 60% in the Property inspector.

11 Use the Pointer tool to reposition the text box so the first word is below the **E** of "Identity" in the movie title.

Adding the cast names

The main stars of the movie are important, too, so you will add those now.

1 Move the cursor between the Wendy image and the silhouette.

2 Type **Mark**.

3 Set the position to X: 534, Y: 8 in the Property inspector.

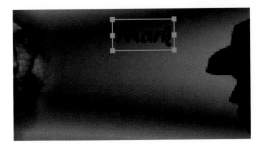

4 Move the cursor away from the text box, and click on the canvas.

5 Type **Wendy**.

6   Set the position to X: 534, Y: 49.

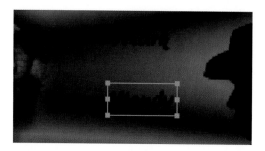

7   With the Pointer tool selected, hold down the Shift key and click on the Mark text and the Wendy text to select both of them.

8   In the Property inspector, set the font size to 16. Your text positions will change slightly because of the change in text size.

9   Select the Text tool again.

10   Click on the canvas to start a new text block.

11   Choose Arial Black again, font size 27, and type **SOUSA**.

12   Set the position to X: 522, Y: 18 in the Property inspector.

13   Click on the canvas again, and type **CARTER**.

14   Set the position to X: 517, Y: 60.

15   Adjust the first names so they appear slightly above the last names.

Styling the text

Now you'll spice up the text of this banner ad a little bit by changing its fill.

1 Zoom in to 300%.

2 Select COMING SUMMER 2009 using the Pointer tool.

3 Open the Fill Color box, and click the Fill Options button.

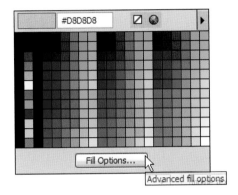

4 Choose Gradient from the Fill Category menu.

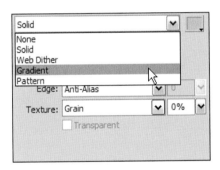

5 Choose Linear from the second Fill Category menu.

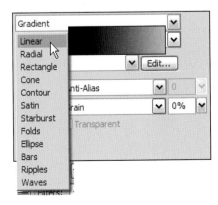

6 Choose White, Black from the third Fill Category menu.

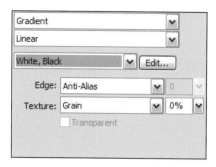

7 Press Enter or Return.

8 Shorten the length of the gradient by dragging the square handle upward.

9 Reposition the circle control handle until it is at the top edge of the text.

Creating a custom style

You're going to use this gradient effect again, so it's a good time to create a custom style.

1 Make sure the text block is still selected, and open the Styles panel by double-clicking on the panel tab or by choosing Window > Styles.

2 Click the New Style icon at the bottom of the Styles panel. The New Style dialog box appears.

3 Deselect all the text properties.

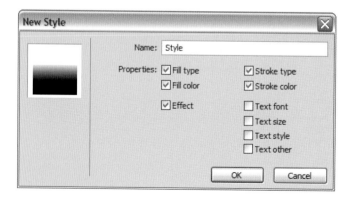

4 Name the style **Movie Text**, and click OK. The new style appears in the Current Document section of the Styles panel.

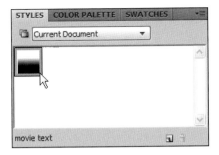

5 Select the Pointer tool.

6 Hold down the Shift key, and select the words Sousa and Carter.

7 Click on the newly created style. The selected text areas receive the same treatment as the COMING SUMMER 2009 text.

● **Note:** Custom styles remain available to any object in the document from which they were created. To make a custom style available to other documents it must be exported. Learn more about exporting styles in the Fireworks Help files.

Styling the first names

You will keep things simple with the first names.

1 In the Layers panel, rearrange the layers so that the names Mark and Wendy are stacked above the two last names.

2 Hold down the Ctrl (Windows) or Command (Mac) key, and select the Mark and Wendy objects in the Layers panel.

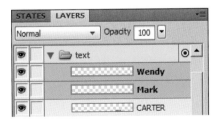

3 Change the text color to **#CCCDDA** in the Property inspector.

4 Select the Scale tool from the Tools panel.

5 Position the cursor just outside of the scaling handles to the right of the text.

6 When the cursor changes to a rotate icon, click and drag upward just slightly.

7 Press Enter or Return.

8 In preparation for the next exercise, hide and lock the text and main layers, and unlock the background layer.

9 Save the file.

Tweaking the background

The background fill has a nice look, but it's a bit dark. You will adjust this now.

1 Select the background rectangle.

2 Click the Add Live Filters (+) button in the Filters category of the Property inspector, and choose Adjust Color > Brightness/Contrast. The Brightness/Contrast dialog box appears.

3 Set the Brightness to **20**, and press Enter or Return.

4 Select the Ellipse tool from the Vector section of the Tools panel.

5 Draw an oval that is 135 pixels wide by 84 pixels high.

6 Set the position to X: 14, Y: 2.

7 Set the Fill category to Solid and the Fill Color to White.

8 Select the Pointer tool.

9 Hold down the Alt (Windows) or Option (Mac) key, and click and drag the oval. This creates a duplicate of the dragged object.

10 Slightly overlap the two ovals, and use Smart Guides to align them at their top edges. Final positions should be X: 14, Y: 2 and X: 126, Y: 2.

11 With both ovals highlighted, choose Modify > Combine Paths > Union.

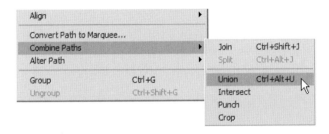

12 In the Property inspector, set the edge to Feather, with a value of 22 pixels.

13 Change the Fill Category to Gradient > Ellipse.

14 Click the Fill Color box to open the Edit Gradient pop-up window. Click the left color swatch, and choose black from the Color Picker.

15 Click the right color swatch, and then click the eyedropper on a bright area of the background rectangle in the file to set the new color.

16 Press Enter or Return.

17 Reposition the gradient to the right, as shown here.

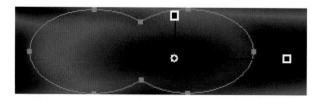

Image positioning

Before you wrap up, you will do a final check on the image locations and save the file.

1 Unlock the main layer.

2 Select the Mark image.

3 Confirm that its position is X: 215, Y: -45.

4 Select the Wendy image.

5 Reposition the image to approximately X: 363, Y: -24 Her face should be a little above vertical center and just to the right of the detective's face.

6 Save the file—you're done!

Review questions

1 What are the primary differences between bitmap masks and vector masks?

2 How do you use the Auto Vector Mask?

3 How do you create a vector mask?

4 How do you create a bitmap mask?

5 How do you create a custom style?

Review answers

1 Bitmap masks are made using selections or using the Brush tool. Using the Brush tool, you can easily edit the mask live on the canvas. Bitmap masks can be applied only to other bitmaps. Vector masks tend to have a higher degree of control and accuracy because you use a path, not a brush, to create them. It's easy to change the fill or stroke of a vector mask. Generating the same type of effect with a bitmap mask can be more time-consuming. Vector masks can be applied to bitmap or vector objects.

2 The Auto Vector Mask can be applied to bitmap or vector objects. Select the object on the canvas, and then choose Commands > Creative > Auto Vector Mask. Choose the type of mask from the dialog box, and then click Apply.

3 To create a vector mask, draw a vector shape, choose Edit > Cut, select the object you want to mask, and then choose Edit > Paste As Mask. You can select the mask in the Layers panel, and change its fill, edge, and stroke properties. You can also use the Pen tool or Subselection tool to edit its shape.

4 You create a bitmap mask in one of two ways:

- Draw a bitmap selection, select the object you want to mask from the Layers panel, and click the Add Mask button in the Layers panel.

- Select the object you want to mask from the Layers panel, and click the Add Mask button in the Layers panel. Select the Brush tool, setting the brush color to black, and then paint on the canvas. As long as the mask object is selected, painting with black will hide pixels from view.

5 To create a custom style, select an object that has Live Filters or fill and stroke attributes applied to it. Click the New Style icon in the Styles panel. Select the properties you want to maintain, deselect those you don't, and name the style.

7 WORKING WITH TEXT

Lesson overview

Fireworks CS4 uses the same text engine as Photoshop and Illustrator, which makes moving or copying between these applications fairly straightforward. Aside from the improved text handling between applications, working with type can be a fun and creative part of your design.

Fireworks has many features normally found in desktop publishing applications, such as kerning, spacing, color, leading, and baseline shift. You can edit text any time—even after you apply Live Filter effects. In this lesson, you'll learn how to do the following:

- Create both fixed width and auto-sizing text blocks

- Edit the text properties

- Use commands to alter text

- Use the transform tools to scale, rotate, and distort text

- Use text as a mask

- Attach text to a path

- Flow text within a vector shape

 This lesson will take about 60 minutes to complete. Copy the Lesson07 folder into the Lessons folder that you created on your hard drive for these projects (or create it now), if you haven't already done so. As you work on this lesson, you won't preserve the start files. If you need to restore the start files, copy them from the *Adobe Fireworks CS4 Classroom in a Book* CD.

Fireworks enables you to use many text formatting features normally found in desktop publishing applications, such as adjusting kerning, spacing, color, leading, and baseline shift.

Text basics

You will be working with a partially complete file for this lesson. The artwork is already in place; you just need to add some text elements.

Creating an auto-resizing text block

1   Browse to the Lesson07 folder, and open the movie_promo.png file.

2   Unlock the Text layer in the Layers panel.

    Text appears inside a **text block** (a rectangle with handles). Text blocks can be either **auto-sizing** or **fixed-width**.

3   Select the Text tool (**T**).

    When the Text tool is active, the Property inspector displays attributes for formatting text, such as font family, font style, size (measured in points), color, alignment, tracking, leading, indent, horizontal scaling, text indent, and paragraph spacing.

    You can also add a stroke color, stroke style, and Live Filters to text. You can change these settings before or after you have added text.

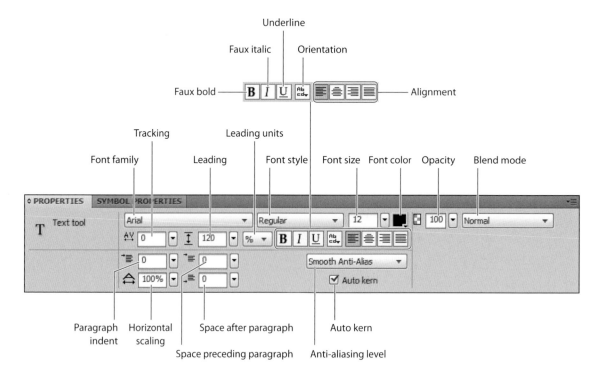

4   In the Property inspector, set the font family to Arial or another san serif font like Helvetica.

5   Set the font style to Regular, font size to 12 points, color to Black, and the Anti-aliasing Level to Smooth.

6   Click anywhere on the canvas.

Auto-sizing text blocks are created by default when you click on the canvas with the Text tool and start typing.

7   Type **He was called crazy, and he was . . . crazy like a fox.**

Note how the text box expands horizontally as you type. It shrinks when you remove text, or adds lines automatically as necessary.

8   Place the text cursor before the letter c in the second instance of the word *crazy*.

9   Press Enter or Return.

He was called crazy, and he was... crazy like a fox.

● **Note:** Fireworks remembers the most recent fonts used by the Text tool, even after you've shut down and restarted your computer. They appear at the top of the font family list. You can change how many recent fonts are displayed by editing the Type preferences.

Creating a fixed-width text block

Fixed-width text blocks allow you to control the width of wrapped text. As you add more text, the box will expand downward. Fixed-width text blocks are created when you drag to draw a text block using the Text tool.

1   Move the cursor away from the first text block.

2   Drag a box that is about as wide as the previous text box. The exact size is not important. This is a fixed-width text block.

3   Release the mouse.

4   In the Property inspector, change the font family to Poplar Std or a similarly bold font.

5   Set the font style to Bold, the font size to 20 points, and the color to #64667F. Leave all the other settings as they are.

6   Type **A Film directed by Robert Legato**. Note that the text wraps to the next line when you reach the right edge of the text box.

When the Text tool is active within a text block, a hollow square or hollow circle appears in the upper-right corner of the text block. The circle indicates an auto-sizing text block; the square indicates a fixed-width text block.

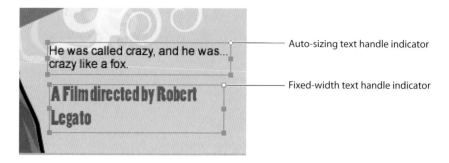

Auto-sizing text handle indicator

Fixed-width text handle indicator

7   Make sure the cursor is flashing in the text block. If it isn't, use the Text tool to click once anywhere in the text.

8   Double-click the hollow control point to change the new text box from a fixed-width block to an auto-sizing block. The text reflows into one line.

Editing text

You must select a text block or specific text within a text block to edit it or change its properties.

1   Select the Pointer tool, and make sure the most recent text block is active. Anything you change within the Property inspector or through text commands will affect the entire text block.

2   Choose Commands > Text > Case Uppercase.

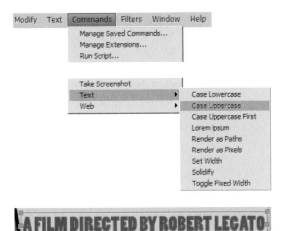

You can change parts of the text in a text block by selecting the text first.

3   Double-click inside the DIRECTED BY text block. This puts you in text-editing mode.

4   Click and drag to select the words *directed by*.

5   Change the font size to 10 in the Property inspector.

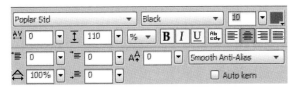

6   Switch back the Pointer tool, and reposition the text to X: 379, Y: 369.

7   Select the first text block.

8   Change the font family to Poplar Std or a similarly bold font.

9   Change the font size to 28, the leading to 110, and the text color to Black (#000000).

10 For now, change the position of the text block to X: 303, Y: 264.

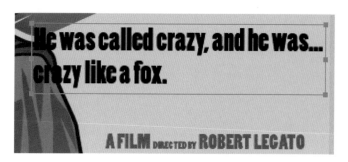

● **Note:** When you edit a text block, all changes during that edit session are considered to be a single step.

11 Save the file.

Flowing text within a vector shape

In many sophisticated page layout applications, such as Adobe InDesign®, you can wrap text around an object. You can achieve this effect in Fireworks CS4 by inserting text within a vector shape.

1   In the text layer, hide the first text object you created, which contains the words *He was called crazy* by clicking the eye icon.

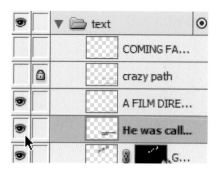

2   Select the Pen tool (⬧).

3 Click once to set a control handle near the shoulder of the detective.

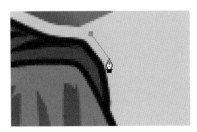

4 Continue clicking with the Pen tool as you follow the contour around the detective's shoulder, and then move across to the right and click to create a straight bottom, straight up the right side, and then back across to the left for the top. Remember, each time you want to change direction, click the mouse to set a control point.

5 Click on the starting control handle to close the path. The final shape should be similar to what you see here.

6 Make both the fill and the stroke of the path transparent by setting their colors to None in the Property inspector.

7 Reveal the crazy text you hid previously.

8 Select both the shape and the crazy text block in the Layers panel.

9 Choose Text > Attach In Path. The text reflows within the vector shape.

● **Note:** If you are having trouble creating this shape, we've created it for you; just unlock and reveal the object called "crazy path."

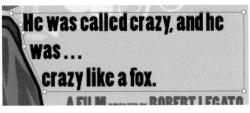

10 Change the Paragraph Indent to 10. This pushes the paragraph 10 pixels to the right from its original starting point.

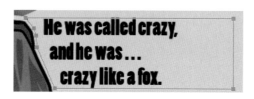

Text attached in a path—or to it—remains editable at all times.

11 Double-click between the comma and the word *and*, and then press Enter or Return.

12 Select the word *fox*.

Note: If you create a shape with one of the Auto Shape tools or the Rectangle tool, you will first have to ungroup the shape before you can attach the text within it. Choose Modify > Ungroup to do this.

13 In the Property inspector, add faux italic styling by clicking the I icon (*I*).

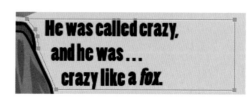

Typography terms

Kerning Adjusts the space between letters based on character pairs. There is strong kerning (more space) between the letters V and A, for example, and no kerning between the letters S and T. You can turn Auto Kerning on or off in the Property inspector.

Tracking Unlike kerning, tracking adds equal amounts of space between all selected characters.

Leading Also known as line spacing, leading is the amount of vertical spacing between lines of type. The word comes from the lead strips that were put between lines of type on a printing press to fill available space on the page.

Horizontal scaling Adjusts the width of each selected character or characters within a selected text box.

Baseline shift Controls how closely text sits above or below its natural baseline. For example, superscript text sits above the baseline. If there is no baseline shift, the text sits on the baseline. To adjust baseline shift, select the actual text (not the text box) and input a value into the Baseline Shift field in the Property inspector.

Paragraph indent Sets the amount of indent for the first line in the paragraph

Paragraph Spacing Sets the amount of spacing before and after a paragraph in a selected text block.

Note: As of this writing, you may end up experiencing text issues when opening a file created in a previous version of Fireworks. Text must be updated when opening a legacy file to minimize issues. Adobe is aware of the problem and engineers are working on a solution. In the meantime, if you experience text alignment issues, be sure to read this blog post: http://blogs.adobe.com/sarthaksinghal/2008/12/cs4_text_woes_workaround.html.

Anti-aliasing

Text anti-aliasing controls how the edges of the text blend into the background so that large text is cleaner, more readable, and more pleasing to the eye. Fireworks examines the color values at the edges of text objects and the background they are on. It blends the pixels at the edges based on the anti-alias settings in the Property inspector.

By default, Smooth anti-aliasing is applied to text. Small font sizes tend to be easier to read when anti-aliasing is removed. Anti-aliasing settings apply to all characters in a given text block.

Anti-alias settings

Fireworks provides four preset anti-alias levels and a custom setting:

- **No Anti-Alias** Disables text smoothing completely. Text is not blended, and anything but horizontal or vertical lines are noticeably jagged. While not ideal for large text, it can actually make text at small sizes (8 point or less) easier to read.

- **Crisp Anti-Alias** Displays a hard transition between the edges of the text and the background. Some blending occurs, but text still appears sharp.

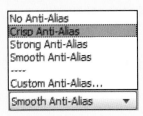

- **Strong Anti-Alias** Creates an abrupt transition between the text edges and the background, preserving the shapes of the text characters and enhancing detailed areas of the characters. Text appears almost bold in comparison to Crisp Anti-Alias.

- **Smooth Anti-Alias** Creates a soft blend between the edges of the text and the background, and is the default for text pasted into Fireworks.

- **Custom Anti-Alias** Choose from these options from the pop-up window that appears:

  Oversampling Sets the amount of detail used for creating the transition between the text edges and the background.

  Sharpness Sets the smoothness of the transition between the text edges and the background.

  Strength Sets how much the text edges blend into the background.

Changing anti-aliasing

The crazy text seems a bit fuzzy against the solid color background. The other pre-set anti-alias settings do not improve matters significantly, so you are going to apply custom anti-aliasing to this text.

1 Select the Pointer tool, and click the crazy text block to make it active.

2 Change the Anti-Alias setting to Custom Anti-Alias, using these values:

- Oversampling: 4

- Sharpness: 96

- Strength: 0

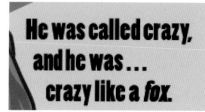

Smooth anti-aliasing

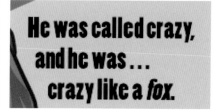

Custom anti-aliasing

Special text effects

There are several kinds of effects and changes you can apply to text to jazz it up.

Attaching text to a path

Attaching text *to* a path—as opposed to *in* a path—lets you put text on an angle, or even follow a curve.

1 Select the Text tool.

2 Set the font size to 24 points in the Property inspector.

3 Click on the canvas, and type **COMING SUMMER 2009**.

4 Select the Pointer tool and drag the text block to X: 327, Y: 237.

5 In the Property inspector, change the horizontal scaling to 109% and the color to #DAEEFA.

Now you can create the path.

6 With the Pen tool (✒), click at the bottom edge of the red banner to set a starting point.

7 Follow the angle of the red banner, and click one more time to set a stopping point for the path.

If you move the cursor again, you will see the Pen tool is still active, dragging a new path segment. You need to disengage the Pen tool and stop the path.

8 Select the Pointer tool and the Path snaps back to a single, selected, segment.

9 Hold down the Shift key, and select the COMING SUMMER 2009 text block. Holding Shift lets you select multiple objects on the canvas.

10 Choose Text > Attach To Path. The text follows the angle of the path (and remains editable).

▶ **Tip:** If the end of your text disappears after you attach it to the path, it means the path is too short for the text. Select the Subselection tool, and drag the end control handle of the path to make it wider. Your text will reappear.

The vertical skew of the text doesn't match the movie title. You will alter this now.

11 With the text object still selected, choose Text > Orientation > Skew Vertical.

12 Reposition the text object, if necessary, and save the file.

Skewing text on an angle

Another way to change the angle of text is to use the Skew tool. In this file, where the cast names are all in separate text blocks, it will be easier to change the angle in this manner rather than attaching each text block to its own vector path.

1 Press the Shift key, and select each actor name.

2 Open the Align Panel (Window > Align).

3 Click the Align Bottom Edge icon (▣).

4 Choose Evenly from the Space area, and click the Space Evenly Horizontally icon (▥).

5 Select the Skew tool (hidden beneath the Scale tool) from the Tools panel.

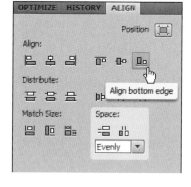

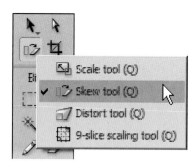

6 Move the cursor over the middle control handle on the right side of the selected block of text.

7 Click the mouse and drag upward until you match the angle of the movie title text.

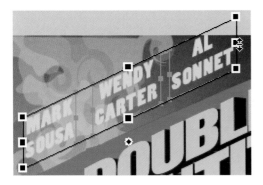

8 Release the mouse to apply the skew.

Using text as a mask

You will add two more special effects to cast names to add some more pizzazz. The first effect you will be creating is a text mask. This kind of effect lets you use the outline of text to mask another object.

1 Select the Rectangle tool (▭) from the Vector section of the Tools panel.

2 Draw a rectangle large enough to cover all three cast-member names.

3 Change the Fill to Gradient > Linear.

4 Select the Fill Color box. and change to the Silver preset gradient.

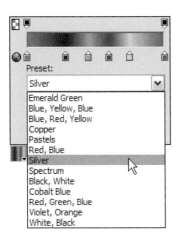 

5 Move the rectangle below the cast names in the Layers panel.

6 Deselect the rectangle.

7 Press the Shift key, and select all three cast names.

8 Choose Edit > Cut.

9 Select the rectangle.

10 Choose Edit > Paste As Mask.

The gradient rectangle is now masked by the text.

11 Click on the text, using the Pointer tool. The gradient control arm appears.

▶ **Tip:** The text remains editable as a mask. Just select the Text tool and click on the text to go into text-editing mode.

12 Drag the square control handle for the gradient to the right so that the gradient runs at approximately the same angle as the text. Drag the square upward to shorten the length of the gradient. You want some contrast between the text and the background.

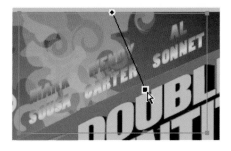

Adding Live Filters to a masked object

Notice the hard, solid shadow on the movie title? You will quickly add a similar effect to the masked gradient, using a Live Filter. Once applied, Live Filters always remain editable so you can always adjust the filter or even remove it, without damaging the original object.

1   If necessary, select the masked rectangle.

2   Click the Add Live Filter (+) button in the Filters category of the Property inspector and select Shadow And Glow > Solid Shadow.

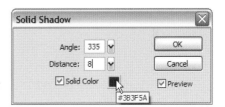

3   Set the Angle to 335.

4   Set the Distance to 8.

5   Select the Solid Color checkbox.

6   Change the Fill color to #3B3F5A. (Incidentally, this color was originally chosen by moving the cursor over the dark blue background and clicking the mouse.)

7   Click OK.

8   Save the file. You're done!

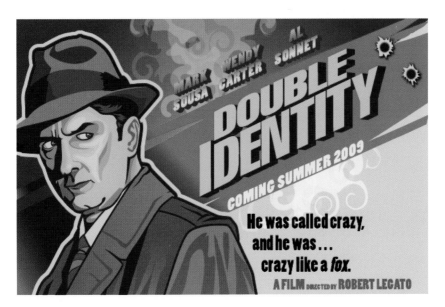

▶ **Tip:** You can tell which object (mask or maskee) is active by looking at the Layers panel. The highlighted object is the one that is active.

Review questions

1 What are the two types of text blocks you can create, and how do you create them?

2 What is anti-aliasing?

3 How do you flow text within a path?

4 What typographic attributes can you control using the Property inspector, and how do these elements affect text?

Review answers

1 You can create auto-sizing and fixed-width text blocks. Auto-sizing text blocks are created by default when you select the Text tool, click the canvas, and begin typing. Auto-sizing text blocks expand in width as you add more text. Fixed-width text blocks are created by dragging out with the Text tool on the canvas first, before typing. Fixed-width text blocks allow you to control the width of wrapped text. As you add more text, the box expands downward.

2 Text anti-aliasing controls how the edges of the text blend into the background so that large text is cleaner, more readable, and more pleasing to the eye.

3 Draw a vector shape using the vector shape tools or the Pen tool. Select both the vector shape and the text, and then choose Text > Attach In Path. If you create a shape with one of the Auto Shape tools or the Rectangle tool, you will first have to ungroup the shape before you can attach the text within it. Select the Auto Shape and then choose Modify > Ungroup to do this. Once text is attached in a path, it still remains editable.

4 Kerning, Tracking, Leading, Horizontal Scaling, Baseline Shift, Paragraph Indent, and Paragraph Spacing can all be controlled from the Property inspector.

- Kerning adjusts the space between letters based on character pairs. You can turn Auto kerning on or off in the Property inspector.

- Tracking adds equal amounts of space between all selected characters.

- Leading, also known as line spacing, is the amount of vertical spacing between lines of type.

- Horizontal Scaling adjusts the width of each selected character or characters within a selected text box.

- Baseline Shift controls how closely text sits above or below its natural baseline. To adjust Baseline Shift, select the actual text (not the text box) and input a value into the Baseline Shift field in the Property inspector.

- Paragraph Indent sets the amount of indent for the first line in the paragraph

- Paragraph Spacing (two settings) sets the amount of spacing before a paragraph (preceding) and after a paragraph in a selected text block.

8 OPTIMIZING FOR THE WEB

Lesson overview

The roots of the versatile Fireworks are in web graphics—be it creating mockups, editing screen resolution images, or optimizing and exporting images to CSS and HTML. And with web graphics, you walk a fine line between quality and file size. Optimization reduces the amount of time a web browser takes to download and display those images.

In Lessons 2, 3, and 4, you learned the basics for working with graphics in Fireworks. Now, you'll apply those skills to creating assets for web pages, and for web page creation itself. You'll learn to do the following:

- Export a single image to a web-ready format

- Determine the optimal web format for a sliced graphic

- Use the Optimize panel and Preview views to optimize images

- Slice up graphics in a web page mockup using the Slice tool

- Create a rollover effect using the Slice tool and interactivity using the Hotspot tool

- Export an interactive mockup of a website

- Export a single page as a standards-based CSS and HTML web page

 This lesson will take about 90 minutes to complete. Copy the Lesson08 folder into the Lessons folder that you created on your hard drive for these projects (or create it now), if you haven't already done so. As you work on this lesson, you won't preserve the start files. If you need to restore the start files, copy them from the *Adobe Fireworks CS4 Classroom in a Book* CD.

Fireworks does many things, but at its roots it is a web graphics application—be it for creating mockups, editing screen resolution images, exporting graphics to Flash, or optimizing and exporting images to CSS and HTML.

Optimization basics

Why optimize images for the web? Simply put, not everyone has the luxury of a high-speed Internet connection, where web pages download at lightning speed. Optimizing images reduces file sizes, decreasing the amount of time it takes for them to be downloaded to a user's computer, regardless of that user's available bandwidth (connection speed). The effective *page weight* (combined file sizes of all assets of a web page, including the page itself) is reduced. It also means they take up less room on the web server.

Optimizing graphics ensures they possess the right balance of color, file compression, and quality. You are trying to get the smallest possible file size (for quick download) while maintaining acceptable quality. Optimizing graphics in Fireworks involves two basic and important components:

- Choosing the best file format for your various graphics

- Setting format-specific options, such as color depth or the quality level

Web graphic formats

To a degree, the file format you choose is a subjective decision, but here are some definitions and general guidelines:

JPEG. For photographic images, JPEG format gives you photorealistic (24-bit) color, and you can control the quality and compression of the file. Higher quality means less compression, which in turn means a larger file size. JPEG is also a *lossy* format, meaning that each time a JPEG file is saved, more of the original image data is discarded. Try to edit files in a lossless format such as PNG, TIFF, or PSD, and then save or export the final file as a JPEG if a JPEG is required. (JPEG format is also used when a composition includes gradients or shadows.)

GIF. GIFs are limited to 256 colors (8-bit), but these colors are customizable. That said, GIF tends to be best for images with solid color, such as logos, line art, or text-based graphics. This format supports transparency settings (indexed transparency) that can give your image the impression of floating over the top of another image or colored background. GIF supports frame-based animation, so you can create simple web-graphic animations. (For complex or large animations, consider using Flash.)

PNG. The PNG format tries to give you the best of both worlds: you can choose among 32-bit, 24-bit, and 8-bit PNG output. A 32-bit PNG allows for 24-bit photorealistic color with 8-bit *alpha transparency,* so you can get more realistic drop shadows or glows around an image or even make the image appear semitransparent on the web page. The image will blend seamlessly with the background color of the web page. (Microsoft Internet Explorer 6 and earlier require special JavaScript to render alpha transparency.) A 24-bit PNG is mildly compressed and lossless, meaning that no image data is discarded when the file is saved. However, unlike JPEG files, you cannot control the compression or quality. The file size is what it is. An 8-bit PNG is much like a GIF, but does not support frame-based animation. Often, you will get smaller file sizes by exporting as PNG-8 rather than GIF. It's definitely worth testing.

● **Note:** Fireworks uses a modified version of the PNG format as its native file format, giving you a great deal of flexibility for editing files. This modified format contains information about layers, states, and effects, and as a result produces a much larger file size than a standard flattened PNG file. For this reason, avoid using a native Fireworks PNG format as part of the real web page. If you want to use the PNG format, the three settings just listed will export out like other image formats.

Saving versus exporting

Fireworks has always made a distinction between the terms *saving* and *exporting*. In general, exporting a file results in a flattened bitmap image; the final file has no layers, vectors, or other unique editable objects. Exporting a file may also include an HTML page, if that option is selected. Exporting a file also uses the information in the Optimize panel to control the exported file format, quality, and color depth.

Saving a file (File > Save) will save the file back into its original format, unless features not supported by that format have been added. For example, a JPEG file is a flat file; it doesn't support additional objects, layers, or editable effects. So if you add these types of features to an open JPEG file, Fireworks will display a warning message about losing the editable features and ask if you really want to save the file back as a JPEG or would rather save it as a Fireworks PNG file. Saving a file bypasses the Optimize panel settings and uses the default settings inherent in the file.

Saving As (File > Save As) can result in a wider variety of formats. You can save in flattened formats such as JPEG, BMP, and GIF or multi-layered Adobe Fireworks PNG files, Adobe Photoshop PSD files, or even Adobe Illustrator® AI files (AI version 8 only).

Other options, such as the ability to maintain XMP metadata, are available for certain files when you save them; however, XMP data is not maintained when you export a file. File > Save ignores the Optimize panel's settings as well, but you can customize those settings by clicking the Options button in the Save As dialog box.

About the Optimize panel

The Optimize panel is located by default in the topmost panel group. If you don't see it, choose Window > Optimize to bring it to the front. You choose the graphic file format you would like to use when exporting a single image file or a selected image slice. Each slice in a design can have completely different optimization settings; this allows for a high level of control over a web page's *weight*.

You can set basic web-optimization settings for a slice using the Property inspector, but you get much more control in the Optimize panel. The Optimize panel also contains non-web formats such as TIFF and BMP, in case your designs—or elements of it—are destined for other uses or mediums.

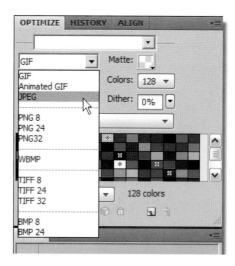

An image with no slices has only one optimization setting for the entire image. An image with one or more slices can have different optimization settings for each slice and one optimization setting for any unsliced areas.

Any changes you make to the optimization settings in either the Property inspector or the Optimize panel will apply to the currently selected slice or slices. If no slices are selected, the optimization setting will apply to the unsliced areas.

The Optimize panel is context sensitive. As you change export formats, the panel displays options for that specific format. JPEG has options only for Matte color, Quality, Selective Quality, and Smoothing.

GIF, Animated GIF, and PNG 8 have options for Matte color, Indexed Palette type, number of colors, Loss, Dither, and Transparency.

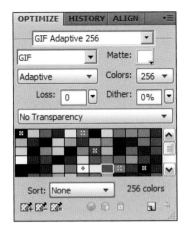 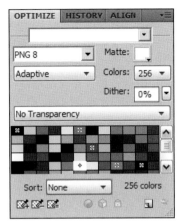

PNG 24 and 32 have no user controls other than the transparency matte color.

The Optimize panel menu contains several features and actions not available in the panel itself, such as the ability to choose interlacing for GIF files, or Progressive JPEG. The panel menu also gives you quick access to the Export Wizard and the Optimize To Size command.

What is matte color?

Matte color—available in all the export formats—is the color Fireworks uses on all areas of the canvas not covered by an object. Changing the canvas color of the document will update the matte color to match, but you can also change the matte color independently in the Matte Color field without affecting the original canvas color. If you need to export the same graphic for use on a variety of web page background colors, this ability can be very helpful. Matte color is also used when you export a GIF or flat PNG file with a transparent background. Set the Matte color to match your web page background color for a more seamless blend on transparent areas.

Optimizing a single image file

You will start by exporting the banner ad you made in Lesson 6 to web-ready format. While this is a simple process, you will get pretty granular in terms of altering image quality, and you will learn about several fundamental features of the Fireworks export process.

Setting preferences

You will be performing some detailed work in this exercise, so before you begin, you need to alter one of Fireworks' preferences.

1 Launch the application.

2 Choose Edit > Preferences (Windows) or Fireworks > Preferences (Mac).

3 Select the Guides And Grids category.

4 Change the Snap Distance to 2 pixels.

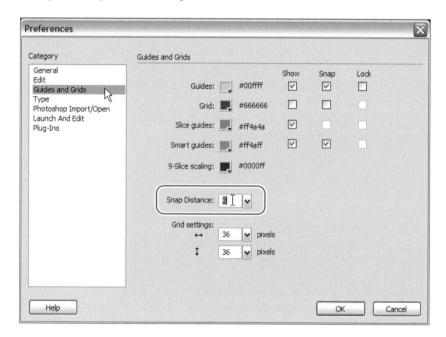

5 Click OK.

Working with previews

1 Choose File > Open, and browse to the Lesson08 folder.

2 Locate and open the movie_banner_final.png file.

A quick glance at the Layers panel tells you this file still has multiple layers and objects. This is fine for editing, but not so fine for the web.

Note: If you do not have the fonts used in the sample file, Fireworks will ask if you wish to maintain appearance or replace the font. For your purposes in this exercise, choose Maintain Appearance.

3 Open the Optimize panel (Window > Optimize, if you don't see it in the panel dock).

At the top of the document window, you see four view options: Original, Preview, 2-Up, and 4-Up. The default view in Fireworks is Original. This is your editing view. The other three views let you preview your design in different formats, based on the settings in the Optimize panel.

4 Click the Preview button.

This view is similar to the Original view, but it applies the settings from the Optimize panel. You cannot edit or select individual objects while in this view.

5 If the file type is set to anything other than GIF, switch it to GIF.

Note: Fireworks uses the last-chosen optimization settings as the defaults for a new or not-previously-exported file.

6 Look closely at the design around the movie title. The gradient effects don't look as smooth as in the Original view. The effects appear *banded*. Zoom in to 150%; the banding is even more apparent.

GIF files can display only up to 256 color values and, as a result, don't do a very good job of rendering many gradient effects.

7 Zoom back out to 100% by double-clicking the Zoom tool in the Tools panel.

8 Look at the bottom left of the document window. Export file information is displayed in this status bar and reads "30.98K 4 sec @56kbps GIF (Document)." (Note that listed file sizes may differ slightly on your own system.) This file-information area, also visible when in Original view, tells you the file size and the download time of the image if it is exported as a GIF file.

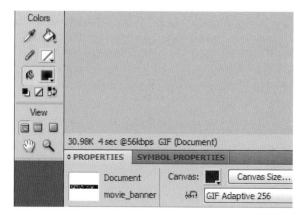

9 Change the Export file format to JPEG – Better Quality in the Optimize panel. Recall that JPEG is usually a much better option for exporting an image with gradients and a wide color range.

10 Zoom in to 150%, and then set the Quality to 80 if it is not already there.

You'll notice that the gradient in the banner ad smoothes out. Equally—if not more—important is the updated information in the status bar of the document window: 17.71K 2 sec @56kbps. The image quality has improved, and the file size has decreased.

17.71K 2 sec @56kbps JPEG (Document)

11 Change to the 2-Up view. The document window splits into two previews of the banner. On the left, the Original view is displayed. On the right, the current optimization settings for the image are displayed. This view is helpful when comparing differences in quality between the original design and an optimized version.

12 Select the Pointer tool, and click on the optimized view. A border appears around that window, indicating it is the active window.

13 Change the Quality setting to 60 in the Optimize panel. You can change the value by typing it in and pressing the Tab key (or Enter or Return) or by dragging the slider. (When you type the value, there is a slight delay before the preview updates with the new quality setting.) The file size decreases to approximately 11.14K.

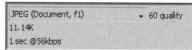

14 Zoom in 150%, if necessary, and compare the two versions of the movie title (Original and Preview). The window views are synchronized, so as you zoom or pan in one window, the other window displays exactly the same view.

● **Note:** If you use the N-Up feature (the ability to dock multiple windows to the application frame), each document window will sport its own Original, Preview, 2-Up, and 4-Up views.

If you study the movie title closely in the Preview version, you will see the background surrounding the text is not as smooth as it is in the Original view. What you see here is the result of the JPEG quality setting. These JPEG artifacts become more visible as you reduce the image quality of the file.

Choosing optimization settings

Comparing the potential export to the original is important, but there are subtle changes in the Optimize panel that can make a big difference to the final exported file. You'll now experiment with the other preview options.

1 Zoom back out to 100%. Even at this 1:1 magnification, the artifacts are still somewhat visible and may be unacceptable to you or a client.

2   Click the 4-Up button. The document window is now split into four previews, the top left one remaining as the Original view.

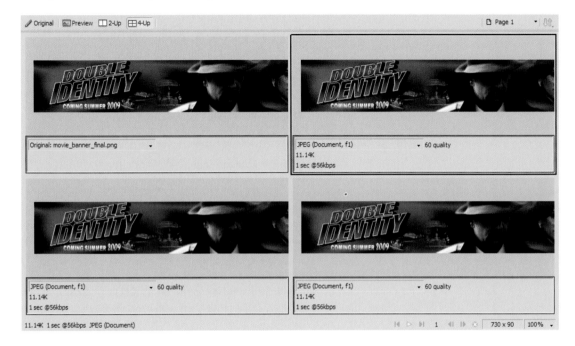

3   Select the bottom-left preview, and change the Quality setting to 80 in the Optimize panel.

4   Select the bottom-right preview, and change the Quality setting to 70.

You now have three different quality/compression previews to compare against the Original view at the top left. By seeing these different versions of the same file, you can quickly determine the best combination of file size and image quality.

5   Zoom in to 150%, and compare the three JPEG versions against the original image. Bearing in mind that none of them will be quite as good as the original, try to determine which of the three is most suitable. The 80% quality looks good, but it's almost 18K. The 60% quality is a great file size, but the artifacts are pretty noticeable. So it looks like 70% could be the winner. But you're not done yet.

6   Change the 70 and 80% previews to 65 and 75%, and inspect them again.

The 75% Quality setting seems to give the best combination of file size and image quality.

7   With the 75% Quality preview selected, click the Original view button. You return to a single view, and your latest settings remain in the Optimize panel.

● **Note:** Understand that, to a degree, this is a subjective choice, especially when you're dealing with small changes in quality or file size. If you're designing a site for an intranet, then you have a little more leeway with your decisions about file size and quality.

Exporting the file

The final step is to export the PNG file as a JPEG file. While a Fireworks PNG file can be displayed by web browsers, it contains information not necessary to a web page image, such as layers, objects, and effects, which can make the file quite large. JPEG files, on the other hand, are flattened images, which you can further reduce in file size by adjusting the quality settings of the file.

1   Choose File > Export.

2   Browse to the Lesson08 folder (or a folder of your own choosing).

3   Change the filename to **movie_banner.jpg**.

4   Choose Images Only from the Export menu, if it is not already chosen.

5   Leave the Include Areas Without Slices and Current Page Only options selected.

6   Click Save (Windows) or Export (Mac).

7   When you return to the canvas, save the file, so that the settings you made in the Optimize panel remain with it, and then close the file.

The Fireworks web tools

To produce compositions in Fireworks that will make their way into a web page, you'll need to be familiar with the available web tools.

There are a number of web-related tools in the Tools panel:

- The three hotspot tools let you draw rectangular, circular, or polygonal shapes over portions of your image to allow those areas of the image to be interactive. When exported with HTML, hotspots link to other web pages or trigger other events on a web page, such as a remote rollover.

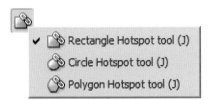

- The Slice tool and the Polygon Slice tool let you cut a larger image into smaller pieces, or just select which parts of a web page prototype will be exported as graphics for a web page.

- The Hide Hotspots and Slices button (⊞) hides slices and hotspots.
- The Show Hotspots and Slices button (⊞) makes slices and hotspots visible.

Creating and optimizing slices

Each web slice has its own optimization settings. Without slices, your image or design has only one optimization setting applied to it, as in the first exercise in this chapter. Individual slices can include interactivity such as image rollovers, hyperlinks, and remote rollovers.

In this section you'll learn several ways to create slices, how to optimize the slices for various types of graphics, and how to name the slices.

Which slice tool do you choose?

You can choose from two slice tool styles: rectangle or polygon. Because web pages are essentially laid out in a grid format, you will most often use the standard Slice tool.

The Polygon Slice tool can be useful if you want a nonrectangular area to be interactive, but this tool uses HTML tables and hotspots as well as slices (the resulting exported file consists of rectangular slices in a table and a polygon hotspot).

You can't have true polygon-shaped images, just like you can't have elliptical-shaped images on a web page. Like it or not, everything ends up as a rectangle, because HTML uses *only* width and height for an image in a web page. If you use a lot of polygon slices, your HTML code can become quite complex and require more CPU processing time, thus slowing down the browsing experience.

Creating slices manually with the Slice tool

You will now use the standard Slice tool to cut up a web page mockup. Accurate slicing is important. If you are going to create manual slices, be sure to zoom to at least 150 or 200% to ensure your slice includes the entire area you want to export.

1 Choose File > Open, and browse to the Lesson08 folder.

2 Open the check_mag_home_start.png file. This is a completed web page mockup.

3 Select the Zoom tool, and zoom in to the upper-left area of the design by dragging the zoom tool around the watch image. This helps to ensure you slice only the graphic and not any surrounding area.

4 With the Pointer tool, select the watch image. Make a note of its dimensions in the Property inspector (237 x 90 pixels).

5 Select the Slice tool, draw a box over the entire watch graphic, and then release the mouse.

A green translucent rectangle appears on top of the watch image.

A slice has three main components: the slice name (user-definable), slice selection handles (for resizing a slice), and the behavior handle for adding interactivity to a slice. Red slice guides will also display, showing you how Fireworks will automatically slice up the rest of the document.

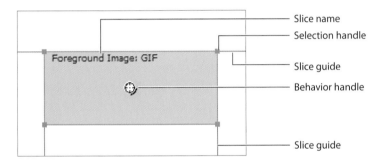

When a slice is created, Fireworks automatically assigns the slice a name, based on the image's filename and future location inside an HTML table-based layout. These names become the actual filenames for the slices when they are exported. They can be fairly cryptic, and likely won't have any relevance to you later in the web production process. We recommend that you custom-name all the slices you create.

6 In the Property inspector, double-click the slice name to select the entire name. Change the current slice name (check_mag_home_start_r2_c2) to **banner_watch**. Note there are no spaces in this name. It's a good idea to use standard web-naming conventions with slices; avoid spaces and special characters, and—ideally—decide on and stick to a system for using upper- and lowercase letters. We keep things nice and simple by putting all web filenames in lowercase.

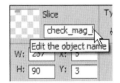

Now even without seeing a thumbnail of the file, you would easily know what this graphic is and where it's supposed to go on the web page.

Adjusting slice dimensions

If this is your first time creating a slice by hand, don't be surprised if you need to tweak the dimensions of the slice. When you are zoomed in, it should be easy to see if the slice is smaller or larger than the image behind it. If you need to make adjustments, you can either use the Pointer tool to resize the slice or change the dimensions numerically in the Property inspector.

● **Note:** With the exception of button symbols, a slice object is not attached to the image below it, so if you reposition the image, you also need to reposition the slice.

Seeing web objects in the Layers panel

Slices and hotspots fall into the category of web objects. When you create either type of web object, Fireworks automatically places them in the Web Layer of the Layers panel. The Web Layer is always at the top of the Layers panel.

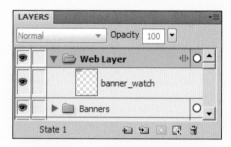

Optimizing a sliced image

This image is also a photo, which means—for optimization purposes—the format should be changed from GIF to JPEG.

1 Open the Optimize panel.

2 Change the Export file format to JPEG.

3 Click on the 2-Up preview button.

Notice that everything except the watch seems grayed out in the preview window. When you have a design with multiple slices, only the selected slice (or slices) will appear normal, so you know what part of your design you are optimizing. Likewise, the optimization information in the preview window is specific to the watch slice.

4   Change the Quality setting to 40. Note that the only area that changes in quality is the watch.

5   Change the Quality setting back to 80.

6   Click the Original view button.

Adding more slices

The beauty of slices is that you can have different formats, and even different optimization settings, in a single design. This gives you the flexibility to truly optimize an entire page design in a single document, rather than having multiple separate image files. You will now add a new slice using an alternate method.

1   Select the Pointer tool.

2   Scroll down near the bottom right of the design, and select the illustration of the race-car driver.

3   Right-click (Windows) or Control-click (Mac) on the image, and choose Insert Rectangular Slice from the context menu. (Note that hotspots can also be created in this manner.)

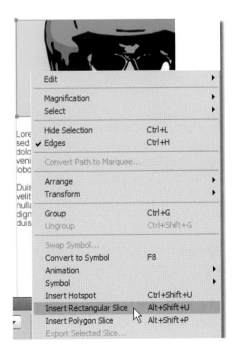

Automatically, a slice is added to the object, based on its dimensions.

4 In the Property inspector, change the slice name to **image_racer.**

Optimizing illustrations

Images that are made up of solid colors need different optimization settings than JPEG to get the best results. For our racer image—the slice you just created—your best format option is either GIF or PNG 8, both of which handle solid color quite well and will compress this image better than the JPEG format. In this exercise, you will discover which of these two formats does the best job.

1 Zoom to 100% so you can see the racer image at its normal size.

2 Switch to the 4-Up preview.

3 Holding down the spacebar, click and drag within any preview window to pan over to the racer.

4 Click on the racer image to make sure it's active.

5 Select the top-right preview window, and set the Export file format to GIF.

6 Make sure the Indexed Palette is set to Adaptive and the Colors to 256.

7 Set the Transparency option to No Transparency.

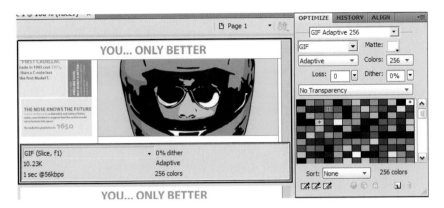

8 Select the preview window at the bottom right, and set the format to PNG 8.

9 Make sure the Indexed Palette is set to Adaptive and the Colors to 256.

10 Set the Transparency option to No Transparency.

11 Note the file size for each. The PNG file should be about 1 KB smaller than the GIF.

PNG 8 is the way to go for this image.

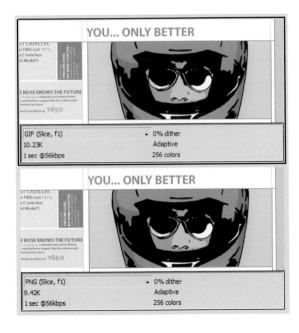

Reducing illustration file size

The main way to reduce file size in GIF or PNG 8 images is to reduce the number of colors.

1 Set all three previews to PNG 8.

2 Select the bottom-left window, and change the number of colors to 128 in the Optimize panel.

3 Make sure the Indexed Palette and Transparency settings are the same as the upper-right preview window.

4 Select the bottom-right window, and change the number of colors to 64 in the Optimize panel.

5 Make sure the Indexed Palette and Transparency settings are the same as the upper-right preview window.

Even at 64 colors, the image looks good, and the file size is pretty reasonable, too.

6 Change the number of colors in the upper-right window to 32.

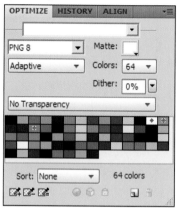

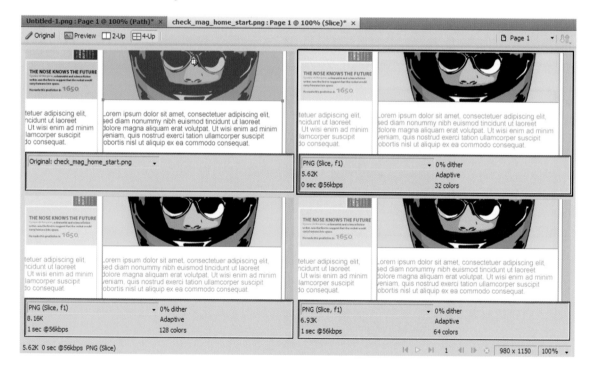

At this setting, the number of colors has been reduced so much that the skin tone is now forced to a more pinkish hue.

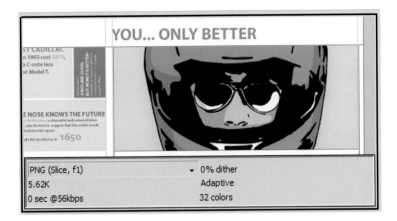

7 Select the 64-color window. To maintain color integrity, you may need to accept a slightly larger file size. You'll need to make decisions about balancing quality and file size for every asset you export.

8 Click the Original view button.

9 Save the file as **check_mag_home_working.png**.

Slicing tricks for working with multiple items

You will add and format the final slices for this design. First you'll use a handy shortcut to create the rest of the slices.

1 Select the Pointer tool.

2 Hold down the Shift key, and click on the remaining five graphics in this layout.

3 Right-click (or Control-click) on any one of the selected objects.

4 Choose Insert Rectangular Slice from the context menu. This time a confirmation box appears, asking if you want to create a single slice or multiple slices from the selected objects.

5 Click Multiple. All five image objects get sliced. They will all have the same optimization settings that you just used in the previous example, and will all be auto-named by Fireworks.

6 Click outside the canvas to deselect all the slices.

7 Hold down the Shift key again, and select just the slices that overlay photos. This will be the movie banner, the large photo of the actor, and the photo of the car.

This time, instead of using the Optimize panel, you'll set basic optimization options in the Property inspector.

8 Change the file format to JPEG – Better Quality in the Slice export settings menu in the Property inspector (below the Type menu).

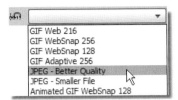

9 Click outside the canvas to deselect all the slices.

10 Hold down the Shift key, and select the navigation area slice and the illustration below the words DATA ADDICT. To make it easier, we've hidden all the slices you *don't* need to worry about in this illustration.

As you'll recall, for the illustration of the racer, you were able to get a nice combination of image quality and file size using PNG 8. These two slices also fall into that category, as they are made up of solid color. The PNG 8 setting is not available in the presets within the Property inspector, so make the changes in the Optimize panel.

11 In the Optimize panel, set the format to PNG 8.

12 Make sure the Indexed Palette is set to Adaptive.

13 Hold down Ctrl (Windows) or Command (Mac), and click on the DATA ADDICT image. (Pressing Ctrl/Command when you click on a slice deselects everything but the targeted slice.)

14 Change the number of colors to 16.

15 Set the Transparency option to No Transparency.

16 Set Dither to 0%.

17 If you see a button titled Rebuild, click it. This will remap the actual colors based on the value in the Colors field.

Optimizing the navigation slice

You have three main colors in this slice—black, white, and blue—but you also have to be aware of any blended pixels used for anti-aliasing.

1 Select the navigation area slice near the top of the page.

2 Switch to the Preview view.

3 Set the number of colors to 256.

4 Select the Zoom tool, and draw a box over the word BLOG. What appeared to be solid blue text at 100% can now be seen to be a mixture of blues, which helps to blend with the black background.

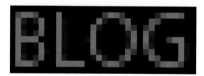

If you look closely at the Optimize panel, you will see that the number of colors for the logo/navigation bar amounts to only 69 in the Optimize panel, even though you specified 256. This is because by default, Fireworks removes any unused colors from the palette. This further reduces the file size of the sliced image.

● **Note:** Should you wish to change the option to remove unused colors, deselect Remove Unused Colors in the Optimize panel menu.

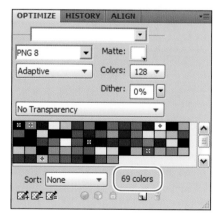

5   Change the color depth to 64. There is no real noticeable change around the word BLOG, even though five colors have been removed.

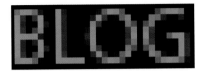

6   Change the value to 32 colors, and you start to see some changes—the blue pixels lose some of their saturation and intensity.

7   Zoom back out to 100%.

8   Change the color depth back to 64.

9   Look closely at the words in the navigation bar, and change the color depth back to 32. Even though you could see changes under extreme magnification, in this image there is no discernable difference when viewed at 100%. Indeed, the point at which the differences truly become noticeable is at eight colors. The blue text is washed out, losing its richness.

10 Set the color depth to 16. This will be the optimization level for the navigation bar. While it may not seem like much, you have reduced the file size of this slice from 6.54 kb to 5.16 kb. In the world of bandwidth and page weight, every little bit (or byte) helps.

▶ **Tip:** If you create a custom optimization setting, you can save it for use at a later time. Just choose Save Settings from the Optimize panel menu.

Naming slices

It's easy to forget to do this, but it's a really good idea, so you will name all those new slices now, before going any further. Remember, you can change the name of any slice directly in the Property inspector.

1 Switch back to Original view, and select the slice that covers the movie banner image.

2 In the Property inspector, change the name to **banner_movie.**

3 Select the slice covering the logo and navigation bar, and change the name to **masthead.**

4 Select the slice covering the actor's photo, and rename it **image_main**.

You'll rename these last two slices in a different manner.

5 Open the Web Layer in the Layers panel if it is collapsed. Collapse the Optimize panel by clicking on the gray bar next to the tabs if you need to free up more room for the Layers panel to expand.

6 Select the slice covering the car.

7 In the Web layer, locate the selected slice.

8 Double-click slice name, and change it to **image_car.**

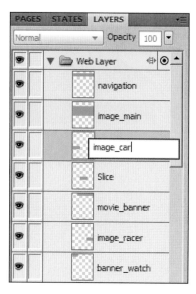

9 Select the slice covering the data illustration, and rename it **image_data.**

10 Save the file.

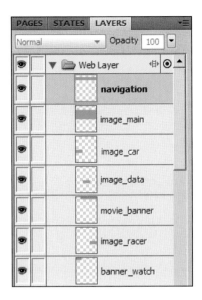

Creating hotspots

You use the various hotspot tools to create hyperlinks within any graphic.

1 Click the Original view button, if you're not already there.

2 Select the Rectangle Hotspot tool ( ).

3 Draw a box around the words FASHION + LIFESTYLE.

The Property inspector updates to display attributes for the hotspot.

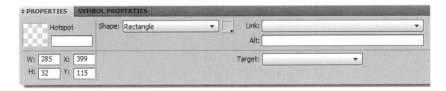

4 In the Link field, type **http://www.adobepress.com/**.

5 Save the file.

6 Choose File > Preview In Browser, and choose your browser from the submenu. Of course, depending on your computer setup, the browsers listed may vary. In our case, the default (Primary) browser was Firefox.

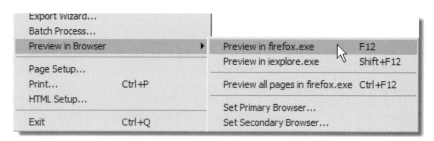

Fireworks launches the selected browser and loads a temporary copy of the web page design.

● **Note:** While the page is a true HTML page, all assets, including any text, are rendered as graphics. These previews are helpful when building site mockups or testing interactivity, but they should not be thought of as exactly how the final web page will look.

7 Click on the FASHION + LIFESTYLE text. If you have a live Internet connection, the browser will load the home page for Adobe Press.

8 Close the browser.

9 Save the file in Fireworks.

If your design has multiple pages (we'll come to that in Lesson 10) you can create links from one page to another using hotspots or slices.

More on the Hotspot tool

Fireworks provides three hotspot tools: the Rectangle Hotspot tool ( ), the Circle Hotspot tool ( ), and the Polygon Hotspot tool ( ). You can quickly access the hotspot tools by pressing the J key. Like all multiple tool icons in the Tools panel, if you keep tapping the shortcut key (or hold down the left mouse button on the tool itself), you will toggle through all the available tools.

The Rectangle and Circle Hotspot tools are pretty self-explanatory, and produce fairly simple HTML code when a file is exported as HTML and Images. The Polygon Hotspot tool creates precise hotspot shapes around irregularly shaped objects. But the amount of HTML markup this type of hotspot produces is significant, so it's best to use the Polygon Hotspot tool sparingly.

Adding interactivity

Much like with hotspots, you can add hyperlinks to slices. If you export from Fireworks in HTML and Images format, the URLs remain with the images. If you export an interactive PDF, again, those links will remain with the slices.

Slices can become *rollover images*, but hotspots cannot. Because a slice is basically a chopped-up part of a large image, you can use built-in JavaScript behaviors within Fireworks to set up a *swap image behavior*. JavaScript rollovers are common in navigation bars. Although the use of CSS and background images is quickly becoming more popular, JavaScript rollovers are quick and easy to do when creating a graphical website click-through. This way, you can easily show a client all the visual interactivity using JavaScript for the mockup, and then deal with coding the CSS rollovers later for the production site.

Here's how to create a simple rollover effect.

1 Open the check_mag_home_working.png file if it's not already open.

2 Hide the slices and hotspots by clicking the Hide Slices And Hotspots button in the Tools panel.

3 Hold down the spacebar, and then click and drag to pan down to the racer illustration.

4 Select the illustration of the racer.

5 Choose Edit > Copy.

6 Open the States panel.

7 Click the New/Duplicate State button to add a new, empty state.

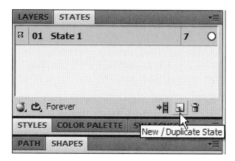

8 Choose Edit > Paste. The racer image appears in the same location as the original, but on (or in) this new state.

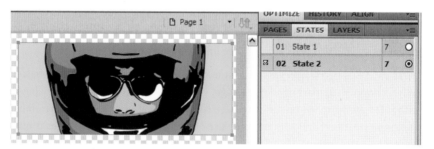

9 Select the racer image on the canvas.

10 Click the Add Live Filter button (+) in the Filters section of the Property inspector, and choose Adjust Color > Invert.

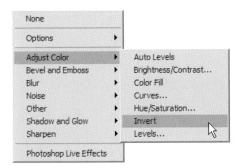

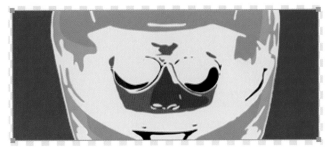

11 Click on State 1 in the States panel. The entire design reappears.

12 Reveal the slices by clicking the Show Slices And Hotspots button in the Tools panel.

13 Click the Behaviors handle on the image_racer slice, and choose Add Simple Rollover Behavior.

14 Click the Preview button at the top of the document window.

15 Move your mouse over the racer image, and watch it change.

16 Save the file.

Exporting composite designs

Fireworks has two main workflows for converting your visual concepts into web pages: you can export as HTML and Images or as CSS and Images.

Exporting HTML and images

The HTML and Images option has been a key workflow feature since the first version of Fireworks. HTML and Images produces table-based HTML layout, which does an excellent job of matching your Fireworks design. It can also include hyperlinks and rollover effects. That is the good news.

Now for the bad news. This table-based layout is very rigid; removing or adding elements to the page using a web page editor like Dreamweaver can cause the table structure—and web page layout—to break. By default, everything in the design is exported as an image, including the text.

From a best-practices perspective, try to avoid table-based layouts for your final websites, and learn how to use CSS for laying out final web pages.

That said, there is a place for this feature in the modern workflow. Many designers use Fireworks' standard HTML capabilities for creating interactive graphical HTML prototypes for client feedback. It's a great way to test ideas and concepts without having to code any HTML right away. The client can request changes on the visual aspects of the design, and you can accommodate them without having to write a single line of HTML code—just update the design in Fireworks and export the file again. After prototype approval, you should code the final pages in a web editor such as Dreamweaver. You will test out this export process now.

1 Open check_mag_home_working.png if it is not still open.

2 Choose File > Export, and browse to the Lesson08 folder.

3 Create and open a new folder in the Lesson08 folder, called **webpage**.

4 Change the Export field to HTML and Images.

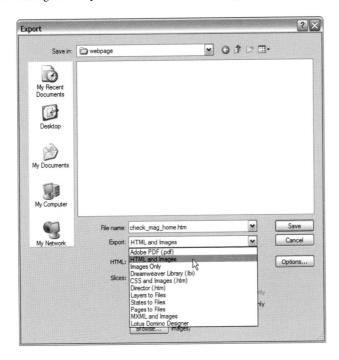

5 Set the HTML field to Export HTML File, and the Slices field to Export Slices. Make sure the following three options are selected: Include Areas Without Slices, Current Page Only, and Put Images In Subfolder.

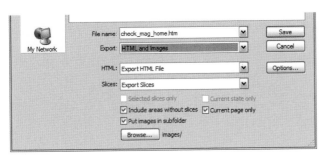

6 Click the Options button, and then the Table tab.

7 Make sure Space With is set to Nested Tables — No Spacers. This setting will maintain the layout without adding multiple transparent spacer images to hold everything together. All other settings can remain at the defaults.

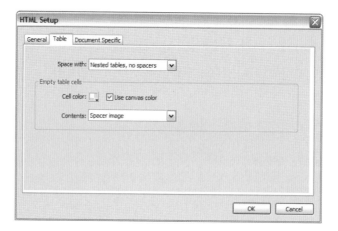

8 Click OK to close the Options dialog box, and then click Export to create your page as HTML.

9 Browse to the webpage folder using Windows Explorer or the Mac Finder.

Inside the folder you will see the web page, check_mag_home.htm, or check_mag_home.html if you've previously altered the default file extension settings, and an images folder.

10 Double-click on the web page to view it in your default browser.

11 Compare the web page to the Fireworks PNG design; you will see they appear very similar, if not identical. You can even click on the hotspot you created earlier over the words FASHION + LIFESTYLE and go to Adobe Press again.

12 Scroll down to the bottom of the web page, and try to select the text. You can't—because it's a graphic. The three blue headings are also one graphic.

13 Close the browser.

14 Open the images folder within the webpage folder.

Twenty-six images—many of which are solid white images—were exported. For the Fireworks-generated HTML to display properly, all these images are needed. In actuality, there are only seven truly necessary images, if you were to build this page in a web editor such as Dreamweaver:

- banner_watch.jpg
- image_racer.png
- image_car.jpg
- image_data.png
- image_main.jpg
- navigation.png
- movie_banner.jpg

Ideally, any text that was exported as images should be re-created as true text within Dreamweaver, and styled using CSS.

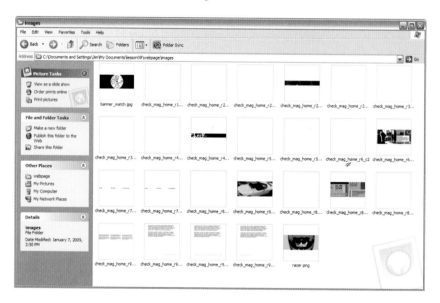

From a mockup perspective, this export is fine: It can show the client how the page will look and even be interactive. However, from a practical, end-user perspective, you would want to build the final web page in a web page editor.

15 Go back to Fireworks, and save the file.

Exporting states

Creating rollovers as you did earlier does present one problem at this time. If you choose to export the HTML and images, including all states, you end up with a bunch of unnecessary extra graphics. You see, Fireworks doesn't just export that one extra rollover image—it exports slices for *every* part of the design in that second state, even if there are no graphics!

The workaround for this is not elegant, but it works, and saves you having to delete many unneeded graphics later on.

1   Reopen the images folder that you exported to previously, and delete all the graphics.

2   Return to Fireworks, and choose File > Export. The export file type should still be set to HTML and Images. If not, go ahead and change it to this setting.

3   Set the Slices field to Export Slices.

4   Make sure that the Include Areas Without Slices, Current Page Only, Put Images In Subfolder, and Current State Only options are all selected.

5   Click Save (Windows) or Export (Mac). When Fireworks asks you if you wish to overwrite any existing files, choose No.

6   When the main document window returns, select the image_racer slice.

7   Right-click (or Control-click) on the slice, and choose Export Selected Slice.

8   Browse to the image folder within the webpage folder.

9   Deselect Current State Only.

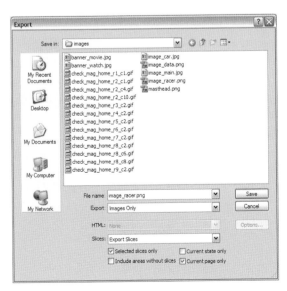

10 Click Save (Windows) or Export (Mac).

11 You will be prompted about overwriting an existing file. Click OK to continue.

12 Test the rollover effect by launching the page in a web browser again.

13 Quit the browser, and then save and close the file in Fireworks.

About CSS

CSS (Cascading Styles Sheets) is the current standard for web page design, and Fireworks has an export workflow to help you in this regard as well. Bear in mind that this doesn't exempt you from learning and understanding how to use CSS in your web page layouts! It is meant as a starting point to producing a more usable web page right from Fireworks.

Here you will learn how to export a CSS-based layout, but we won't be discussing the fine details of Cascading Style Sheets. Entire books have been written on CSS and its use, and this book does not pretend to be one of them. To begin with, we're going to give you a lot of preparatory information, explaining the logic behind the CSS and Images export feature. If you want to just try the export, you can skip down to the next section, "Exporting CSS and images."

Here are some design concepts to keep in mind if you plan to export a CSS-based layout:

- **Only text, rectangles, and image slices are exported.** To export as CSS and images, any images you want as part of the web page must be sliced. Any text you wish to remain as true HTML text should *not* be sliced. Fireworks will create an HTML web page, using DIV tags to contain the text and images, according to the slices, rectangles, and text it finds in the design. A Cascading Style sheet is also created, to handle positioning of the DIVs and styling of the text.

- **Text, rectangles, and image slices are all treated as rectangular blocks.** The exporter (also called the export engine) examines the size of text blocks (the actual bounding box, remember, *not* the width/height of the text itself), rectangles, and slices in order to create the proper spacing between the elements. It also determines the logical placement of columns and rows, based on the position of the design elements in your file.

  Text blocks can be deceiving, because the rectangle area that defines the text block may actually be much larger than the text, causing two objects to overlap, as seen here.

Lorem ipsum dolor sit amet, consectetuer adipiscing elit, sed diam nonummy nibh euismod tincidunt ut laoreet dolore magna aliquam erat volutpat. Ut wisi enim ad

- **The exporter must be able to interpret where the columns and rows of objects exist.** Even though you are not using tables for layout, keep thinking in that grid-like fashion. Make it easy for the export engine to figure out where logical containers—such as a header, a sidebar, a main content area, and a footer—would go.

What is a DIV tag?

The HTML DIV tag is used for defining a section of your document. It acts as a container for other elements of a web page. With the DIV tag, you can group HTML elements together and format them with CSS. For example, you could have your header section, navigation section, and main content sections wrapped in their own separate DIVs.

Fireworks will wrap text and images inside DIV tags based on the layout, which is why placement of design elements is critical when exporting in CSS and Images format. In order for Fireworks to lay out the page using its CSS layout engine, it is important that slices do not overlap other slices, and that text areas do not overlap slices.

- **Use rectangles to create a specific DIV around objects.** If you draw a rectangle around specific elements, Fireworks will understand that the objects inside the rectangle should be in their own DIV container in the final CSS layout. For example, if you wanted to guarantee that each of the lower columns in the check_mag_home_working.png file were given their own DIV containers in the final layout, you could draw a rectangle around each column. This helps the exporter decide what to do. In the following illustration, we've drawn a rectangle around the left side column. Notice how all bounding boxes of the design elements in the column are *inside* the large rectangle. There are no overlaps.

If Fireworks encounters any overlaps, a warning message will appear, telling you where the first overlap was encountered, and that the export is switching to Absolute Positioning mode. This mode is still CSS-based, but Fireworks places each object at an exact location in the browser window—the elements in the page are fixed in place. If you later wish to add text in a web page editor, or other content using a content-management system, the other page elements won't move to accommodate the extra content.

The CSS and Images export feature will export out only sliced images, and generate a CSS-based, HTML web page layout. Interactive elements such as hotspots or rollover effects will be ignored; Fireworks will display a warning message to remind you of that fact. Interactive elements would have to be added using your web page editor.

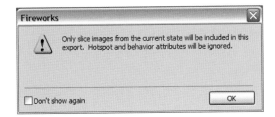

Exporting CSS and images

You will test out the CSS and Images export using a different version of the same design you have been working with. This version has all the slicing and optimization set for you.

1 Save and close any other files currently open.

2 Choose File > Open, browse to the Lesson08 folder, and open the file called check_mag_home_css.png.

▶ **Tip:** To check for overlaps in your design, press Ctrl+A (Windows) or Command+A (Mac) to select all the objects in the design. This will show you if any bounding boxes (text or graphics) are colliding.

Zoom out far enough that you can see the entire design. Notice the layout is gridlike. There are distinct gaps between the various content areas. While these gaps are not necessary for a successful CSS and Images export, they make it easier for someone new to the feature to understand what is going on. The important thing to remember is to avoid overlaps between slices, rectangles, or text.

The basic structure of web pages is, essentially, some sort of grid. Sometimes that grid is not very obvious and sometimes there are objects in DIV containers that sit *above* the main page layout (such as a pop-up slideshow or a Flash video), but these are in addition to the basic page structure.

3   Select the banner_watch slice. In the Property inspector, notice that the Type field says Foreground Image.

You can actually set three different types of slices:

- **Foreground Image**—Sets the images in the web page to be inline images, which are part of the flow of the document.

- **Background Image**—When this type is selected, you can set other CSS-related attributes for background images, such as repeat, scroll, vertical position, and horizontal position. This slice type does not work with the HTML and Images export, only when exporting with CSS.

- **HTML**—Allows you to add true HTML code to a slice, rather than just an image. This slice type does not work with the CSS and Images export, only when exporting HTML.

All the slices in this file are Foreground Image slices, which is fine for this exercise.

4 Choose File > Export, and browse to the Lesson08 folder.

5 Create a new folder called **csswebpage**.

6 Open that folder and create another new folder, this time called **images**.

7 Choose CSS and Images from the Export menu in the Export dialog box.

8 Make sure the option Put Images In Subfolder is selected. The path to this folder should be the new "images" folder you just created. If it looks like Fireworks is pointing to another images folder (like the one from the last export), click the Browse button and locate the correct images folder.

9 Click the Options button.

For CSS export, the General tab is the only one you need to concern yourself with. You can tell Fireworks whether to write the CSS to a separate file, choose an existing image to set as a background image, and also set the page alignment.

10 Ensure that Write CSS To An External File is selected.

11 Make sure the Page Alignment field is set to Center.

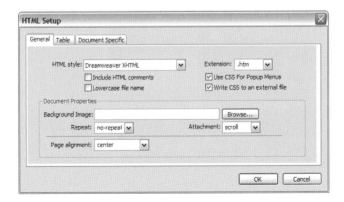

12 Click OK, and then click Save (Windows) or Export (Mac).

A warning box appears telling you this file uses nonstandard web fonts, and recommends you either add a slice over that text to export it as a graphic, or cancel the operation and change the fonts to more common ones.

▶ **Tip:** To learn more about which fonts are safe to use on the web, check out Code Style's Most Common Fonts survey results at www.codestyle.org/css/font-family/sampler-CombinedResults.shtml.

This is good information to note. Web browsers rely on the user's fonts for displaying text on a page, so if you have chosen an unusual font, the person visiting your site may not see what you had intended. Instead, they may end up with Arial, Helvetica, Times New Roman, or some other more common font.

This time, though, by agreeing to use whatever non-standard fonts you like, you will laugh in the face of the World Wide Web. Well, maybe a quiet chuckle will do.

13 Click OK to continue with the export.

14 Open the csswebpage folder in Windows Explorer or the Mac Finder.

15 You will see check_mag_home_css.htm (or check_mag_home.html if you changed the file extension preferences), check_mag_home.css, and the images folder containing seven images.

16 Double-click on the web page to open it in a web browser.

The page opens, centered in the browser window. Other than that, it seems pretty much like the HTML export. Or is it?

17 Run your mouse over the racer image. No image rollover occurs. When you export as CSS and images, any JavaScript behaviors—such as image rollovers—are ignored in the export.

18 Scroll down to the bottom of the page, and try again to select the text. This time you *can*. The CSS Export script has recognized these unsliced areas as text and has exported them as such. Even the blue headings have been exported as text.

If you were to open the page in Dreamweaver and select the text, you would see that the text is within paragraph tags, and is styled using a CSS class.

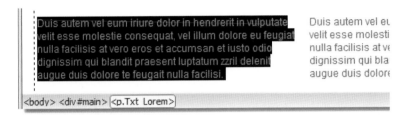

19 Save and close the file.

Updates to the CSS Export feature

It's obvious that the Adobe Fireworks development team is aware of the need for a CSS export solution. The CSS export script that comes with Fireworks CS4 is a good start, but it's not perfect. To that end, in late 2008 Matt Stow (www.mattstow.com), a web- and user-interface designer who specializes in designing and developing accessible, standards-compliant websites, worked with the development team to produce a more enhanced CSS Export Script feature.

The main improvements are:

*   Creating semantic markup is made easier by tagging text objects.

*   All font sizes are created using percentages, to allow for user text resizing in all devices and browsers.

*   DIV elements with heights now also have a min-height equivalent to allow for varying amounts of content and user text resizing.

*   Multiple paragraph elements are now created from a single text object where appropriate, as opposed to using breaks.

*   There is an improved, more flexible library of HTML component symbols, including a List Item symbol to create unordered lists.

*   DIVs with all border placements and sizes now output at the correct size and are positioned more correctly.

You can download the new script and assets and read Matt's detailed tutorial by visiting the Adobe website at www.adobe.com/devnet/fireworks/articles/standards_compliant_design.html.

For your convenience, these files can also be found in the Lesson08 folder of this book's CD.

The tagging capabilities alone open up a lot more control over text. The shining star of the new assets is the List Item symbol, which is ideally suited to creating a horizontal navigation list.

Review questions

1 Why should images be optimized for the web?

2 What are the two types of web objects you can create in a Fireworks design, and how do they differ?

3 How do you create an image slice?

4 What are the main workflows for generating web pages from Fireworks?

Review answers

1 Optimizing graphics ensures that they are set to a suitable format and possess the right balance of file size, color, file compression, and quality. You are trying to get the smallest possible file size (for quick downloads) while maintaining acceptable quality in the image. Optimizing graphics in Fireworks involves choosing the best file format for a graphic and setting format-specific options, such as color depth or quality level.

2 Slices and hotspots are the two main kinds of web objects you can create in Fireworks. Both types of web objects can have URLs added to them for interactivity.

Slices let you cut up a larger design into smaller pieces and individually optimize each slice to get the most suitable combination of file size and image quality. Slices can also be used to generate rollover effects.

Hotspots create an interactive area within an image. They do not cut up an image like slices do. They were commonly used to create image maps—a single image that had multiple hyperlinks applied to it in different areas of the image. Hotspots can also be used to trigger rollover events on the web page.

3 You can create an image slice in one of two ways:

- You can right-click (or Control-click) an object in your design, and then choose Insert Rectangular Slice.

- Using the Slice tool, you can manually draw a slice on top of an object or objects within the design.

4 There are two main workflows for exporting complete HTML pages:

- **File > Export > HTML and Images.** This exports rigid, table-based design consisting entirely of graphics. Even the text is exported as graphics. Pages created this way are difficult to edit, because removing or adding new elements to them using a web page editor can break the layout. However, this export is ideal for creating interactive prototypes of a web page or a website. While not suitable for a final website, the HTML pages can show the client how the site will look, and can also support rollovers and hyperlinks, so a client can interact with the prototype and request changes or approve a design before any work needs to be done on the coding side of the project.

- **File > Export > CSS and Images.** This option can generate a more standards-based, editable web page by creating the layout using Cascading Style Sheets rather than tables. Moreover, this export option recognizes text, and exports it as true HTML text. With a working knowledge of CSS, these pages are easier to edit and more flexible in terms of adding new elements within a web page editor.

9 USING SYMBOLS

Lesson overview

Symbols are one of the great time-saving features in Fireworks. They've been around since the beginning of the application. Symbols can contain multiple objects within a single asset while still giving you quick access to editing those objects. They are a great option for reusing common graphical elements in a design—like a logo or a button. Symbols can contain text, vectors, and bitmaps, each with their own Live Filter attributes.

In this lesson, you'll learn how to do the following:

- Create and edit a graphic symbol

- Create and edit an animation symbol

- Create and edit a button symbol

- Save a symbol to the common library

 This lesson will take about 60 minutes to complete. Copy the Lesson09 folder into the Lessons folder that you created on your hard drive for these projects (or create it now), if you haven't already done so. As you work on this lesson, you won't preserve the start files. If you need to restore the start files, copy them from the *Adobe Fireworks CS4 Classroom in a Book* CD.

Symbols are one of the great time-saving features in Fireworks. They are a great option for reusing common graphical elements in a design—like a logo, or a button.

What are symbols?

A symbol is a master version of a graphic or of a collection of graphics.

A symbol is essentially a self-contained document within a document. You have all the editing capabilities at your fingertips that you would have for a complete design, but all the assets of the symbol itself are kept together.

When you place a symbol on the canvas, you're actually placing a linked copy of the symbol, which is known as an *instance*. When you edit the original *symbol object,* the linked *instances* on the canvas automatically change to reflect the edited symbol.

You can also edit any symbol instance on the canvas, changing size, color, opacity, or adding Live Filters, without altering the original symbol. For example, you might have a fairly large image of a company logo. If you convert that image into a symbol, you can simply drag an instance onto the canvas and scale it down, without affecting the original large version.

Another advantage to symbols is their time-saving characteristics. Instead of having to locate the original file each time you need a logo, you can turn it into a symbol and make it quickly available from the Document Library panel. This is obviously a big advantage if you regularly reuse objects.

While you can build your own, Fireworks also comes with a wealth of predesigned symbol objects that you can use as part of your designs or for jump-starting your own creative talents.

Three main types of symbols are available within Fireworks: graphic, button, and animation symbols. There is also an enhanced graphic symbol type referred to as a *component symbol.* In this lesson, you will be creating and editing the three standard symbol types.

In this lesson, you'll be taking a bit of a break from the Double Identity assets. Instead, you will be working with and creating some generic symbol assets that can be used for websites or application mockups.

Graphic symbols

A graphic symbol is a commonly used asset in Fireworks. It is a static, single-state symbol that can be used over and over again throughout a document (or other documents as well, depending on how you set it up). Use a graphic symbol if you do not require built-in animation or multiple states.

Creating graphic symbols

In this exercise, you will convert a simple logo graphic into a graphic symbol.

1 Open the file called baretree_logo.png.

2 Make sure rulers and tooltips are active (View > Rulers and View > Tooltips).

3 Press Ctrl+A (Windows) or Command+A (Mac).

4 Choose Modify > Symbol > Convert To Symbol.

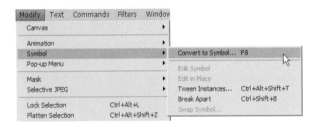

5 Name the symbol **baretree logo**.

6 Make sure Type is set to Graphic, and leave the options deselected.

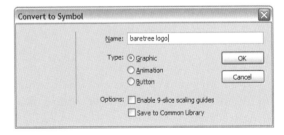

7 Click OK.

8 Open the Document Library panel. The new symbol is displayed there.

Saving to the Common Library

When creating a new symbol, saving it to the Common Library will remove the object from the canvas. You will need to locate the newly created symbol in the Custom Symbol folder of the Common Library panel and insert it back into your document.

The advantage to enabling the Save To Common Library option in the Convert To Symbol dialog box is that the new symbol becomes available to *any* document you work on, not just the current document.

You can always add a symbol to the Common Library after it has been created; for details, see "The universal Common Library."

Once a symbol is created, you will notice a faint blue plus sign (+) in the middle of the graphic on the canvas. This indicates that the graphic is a copy—or *instance*—of the symbol.

The universal Common Library

When you create a symbol, it is linked only to the document where it was created. If you open or create another document, you won't see your newly created symbol in the Document Library. After you have gone to all the trouble of creating those symbols, you may want them available for use in other designs, without having to first open a file, copy the instance on the canvas, and then paste it into a new document. This is where the Common Library comes to the rescue. The Common Library makes symbols easily accessible for any design.

1 In the Document Library panel, select the baretree logo symbol.

2 Choose Save To Common Library from the Document Library panel menu.

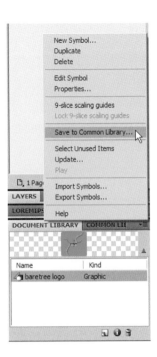

A Save As dialog box (or Save dialog box on the Mac) will open, and should be pointing to the Custom Symbols folder, where all user-created custom common symbols are located by default. This folder displays automatically in the Common Library panel, so it's a good idea to save it there.

There is a specific structure to symbol file names, starting with the symbol name and appended with the symbol type (graphic, animation, or button), preceded by a period.

3   Click Save.

Adding a graphic symbol to a document

You will now add this graphic symbol to a partially completed web page design.

1   Open the file simple_page.png from the Lesson09 folder.

2   Open the Common Library panel (Window > Common Library).

3   Choose the Custom Symbols folder. You will see the baretree logo symbol in the panel.

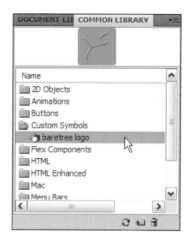

4   Drag and drop the symbol onto the canvas. You now have an instance of the symbol of the canvas—a rather large instance, actually.

5   Select the Scale tool ( ) from the Tools panel.

6   Drag inward from the bottom-right corner of the logo until the instance is approximately 100 x 98 pixels.

7   Press Enter or Return to commit to the new size.

Note: You need to drag a symbol only once from the Common Library; once it's been dragged from the Common Library panel onto a document, it becomes part of that file's Document Library.

8   Use the Pointer tool to reposition the instance of the logo to the upper-left corner, at a position of X: 10 and Y: 10.

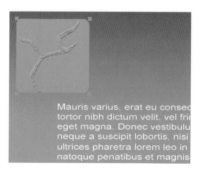

9 If necessary, open the Document Library panel.

Now you'll add another instance of the same symbol, but don't worry—it won't end up looking repetitive.

10 Drag a new instance of the baretree logo from the Document Library panel onto the canvas.

11 Select the Scale tool again, and resize the new instance until it is only 70 pixels wide.

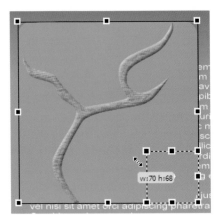

While in Scaling mode, you can reposition the object.

12 Move the mouse on top of the object. The cursor changes to a four-pointed move icon. Be sure *not* to drag the center control handle—that circle controls the rotation axis of the object.

13 Drag the object to the lower-left corner, 10 pixels from the right and bottom edges (X: 10, Y: 340).

● **Note:** If you move an object while in scaling mode, you will not see any tooltips to indicate the position of the object.

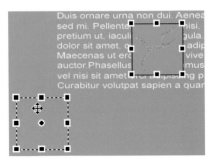

Editing graphic symbols

Some attributes—like size, opacity, blending mode, and Live Filters—can be applied to individual instances on the canvas. Changes to a selected instance do not affect other instances on the canvas. Editing the symbol, however, changes properties in all instances of the symbol.

In this exercise, you're going to add another graphic element to this admittedly rather bare logo.

1   Using the Pointer tool, double-click on the larger of the two baretree instances. Everything but the instance fades slightly, and a breadcrumb bar appears above the document window.

You are now in a symbol-editing mode called Edit In Place mode, a feature that has been available in Adobe Flash for quite some time. You can also enter this mode by choosing Modify > Symbol > Edit In Place. The breadcrumb trail tells you how far you have drilled down into a symbol. Changes made to a symbol in this mode are instantly reflected in all the linked instances on the canvas.

You can exit in-place editing and switch back to the main design by clicking on the top-level breadcrumb (Page 1) or by double-clicking anywhere on the canvas except the active symbol.

2   Choose File > Open.

3   Browse for leaf.png. This image comprises three vector objects.

4   Press Ctrl+A (Windows) or Command+A (Mac) to select all the objects.

5   Choose Modify > Group to group the three vectors together. This will make it easier to move and manage the image. You can always ungroup it later, should you need to edit it again.

6   Choose Edit > Copy.

7   Return to the simple_page file. You should still be in the Edit In Place symbol-editing mode.

8   Choose Edit > Paste. Note that the smaller instance also updates with the pasted leaf.

9   Zoom in to 200%.

10 With the Scale tool, drag inward from the bottom-right corner to resize the leaf to about 25 pixels wide.

11 Press Enter or Return to lock in the new size. If you zoom back out, you will see the smaller logo also has the leaf.

12 Reposition the leaf to X: -1, Y: 0. When you are in symbol-editing mode, the X and Y coordinates are relative to the registration point in the center of the symbol.

13 Click on the background rectangle of the logo.

14 In the Property inspector, change the Fill Category to Gradient > Radial. The outer part of the gradient should be the original green fill color; the central part will be black. You need to change the inner color from black to yellow.

15 Click the Fill color box in the Property inspector, and then click the black color swatch in the Gradient pop-up window. Choose a rich yellow (#FFFF00) from the color picker.

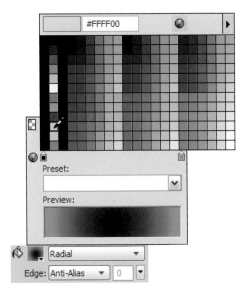

16 Reposition the gradient so that it is centered under the leaf.

17 Adjust the length of the gradient so that the rectangle fades to a solid green at the right side, similar to what's shown here.

The effect is applied to both instances.

18 Click on Page 1 of the breadcrumb trail to return to the main design.

19 Save the file as **simple_page_working.png**.

Isolation Mode

Another option for editing symbols is referred to as *isolation mode*. This is the default mode for any symbol to which the 9-Slice Scaling Guides option has been applied. You can access isolation mode for any symbol, though, by choosing Modify > Symbol > Edit Symbol. The symbol remains on the canvas, but all other objects are hidden from view. If you have a full design, this mode may make it easier for you to edit aspects of symbols without any distractions.

Adding prebuilt symbols from the Common Library

The Common Library holds a wealth of prebuilt symbols you can use for your designs or as a starting point for your own symbols. The Common Library does not become populated with symbols until a document is open in Fireworks.

To familiarize yourself with this useful feature, you will add a mockup of a search box using a rectangle and a prebuilt symbol. Make sure you're back on Page 1 in your document.

1 Open the Common Library panel.

2 Scroll down until you see the Web & Application folder.

3 Double-click on the folder icon (Windows) or click the disclosure triangle (Mac) to open the folder. If the Common Library panel returns to the top, scroll back down to the now-open folder.

4 Locate the Search symbol.

5 Drag the symbol—either the graphic itself or its name—onto the canvas.

The instance of a magnifying glass is fairly large and needs to be resized.

6 With the Scale tool, drag a corner scaling handle inward until the image size is about 20 pixels.

7 Press Enter or Return to lock in the new size.

8 Select the Pointer tool, and reposition the magnifying glass to X: 720, Y: 12.

9 Select the Rectangle tool, and draw a rectangle that is 200 pixels wide by 20 pixels high.

10 Fill the rectangle with white, and give it a black, 1-pixel hard stroke.

11 Use the Pointer tool to position the rectangle at X: 520, Y: 12.

You now have a mockup of a search bar.

12 Save the file.

Button symbols

Button symbols serve a very specific purpose: making button rollover states for navigation buttons.

Button symbols are a very efficient way to generate up to four visible states for a button (Up, Over, Down, and Over While Down) and adding a hyperlink to them. Almost any graphic or text object can become a button. After you have created a single button symbol, you can reuse it again and again for navigation. Each instance of a button symbol can also have its own custom text, URL, and target without breaking the two-way symbol–instance relationship.

A button instance is self-contained. All the graphic elements and states are kept together, so as you move the Up state of a button on the canvas, the other states and the button slice move with it.

When you export a button, Fireworks can generate the JavaScript necessary to display it in a web browser. In Adobe Dreamweaver, you can easily insert JavaScript and HTML code from Fireworks into your web pages or into any HTML file (very handy for interactive HTML prototypes). For production sites, most designers opt to create the code and JavaScript by hand or by using Dreamweaver's behaviors.

Creating button symbols

You can create a button from any object, but usually the button starts out as a vector shape or a bitmap object.

1 Select the Rectangle tool, and draw a rectangle that is 100 pixels wide by 20 pixels high.

2 Use the Pointer tool or the Property inspector to position the rectangle at X: 80 and Y: 115.

3 Open the Styles panel, and choose Plastic Styles from the Styles list.

4 Choose the style Plastic 044. The rectangle should take on a glassy, green style.

5 Choose Modify > Symbol > Convert To Symbol.

6 Name the symbol **navButton**.

7 Change Type to Button, and click OK.

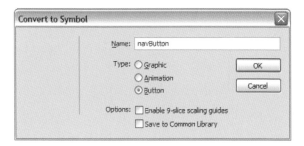

You're now back on the main canvas. Fireworks automatically adds a slice to a button symbol, because button symbols are mainly used for rollover effects, and a slice allows for image swapping to other button states.

To maintain a good-quality gradient, you will set the export options for this file to JPG or PNG-24.

8 Open the Optimize panel and, if necessary, choose PNG-24 from the Export File Format list.

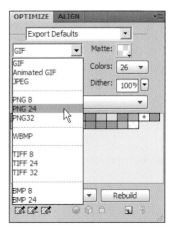

Editing a button symbol

To start, a button symbol (like a graphic symbol) also has only one state. Buttons also need text labels. The slice created by Fireworks tries to include all visual properties of the button, some of which are not very easy to see. You will add text to the button, add another state, and edit the slice size manually.

1 Double-click the button slice. All objects other than the button are grayed out.

2 With the Text tool selected, in the Property inspector, set the font family to Arial, font style to regular, size to 12 points, and color to Black.

3 Set the text alignment to Center Alignment and the anti-aliasing level to No Anti-Alias.

4 Click on the canvas right on top of the rectangle, and type **Funding Options.**

● **Note:** The expectation with button symbols is that you will be creating one or more graphical navigation buttons, with different visual appearances to reflect the state of the button. So it is important to determine what the longest string of button text will be, in order to set a font size that will allow the various button-text strings to fit comfortably within the button shape.

5 Select the Pointer tool, and drag over both the rectangle and the text block to select them.

6 Open the Align panel, and click the Align horizontal center (呂) and Align vertical center (吕) icons to position the text within the rectangle.

While we're here, let's create a rollover state.

7 Click away from the button using the Pointer tool.

8 In the Property inspector, choose Over from the State menu. The button disappears.

9 Click the Copy Up Graphic button. This adds a duplicate of the Up state to the Over State.

10 Select the rectangle using the Pointer tool.

11 Open the Path panel, and select Reverse Gradients.

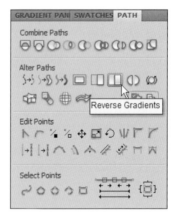

12 Select the text block.

13 In the Property inspector, change the font style to Bold and the color to White.

14 Click the Page 1 breadcrumb to go back to the main canvas.

CSS rollovers

Many web designers now use background images and CSS to create a button rollover effect, because the text in a CSS rollover remains true HTML text. However, button symbols can't be beat for creating interactive HTML prototypes.

Adding more buttons

Most sites need more than a single navigation button, so you will add a few more.

1 Make sure the Pointer tool is selected and the button slice is active.

2 Hold down the Alt (Windows) or Option (Mac) key, and use the Pointer tool to drag the button to the right, until it snaps to the right edge of the original button. (Holding down Alt/Option creates a copy of the selected object.) Let the Smart Guides help you position the new button directly next to the first button.

3 Select both buttons, and then repeat step 2 twice, so you have six buttons.

All six buttons currently have the same text. That's not much help!

4 Select the leftmost button. The words *Funding Options* appear in the text box in the Property inspector.

5 Change the text to **Home**, and press Enter or Return.

The button text updates.

6 Select the second button.

7 Change the button text to **Our Mission**, and press Enter or Return.

8 Skip the third button, as it already says **Funding Options**.

9 Select the fourth button, and change the text to **Events**.

10 Change the text for the fifth button to **Contact** and the sixth button to **Gallery**.

Take this time to rename the slices as well.

11 Click on the Home button and, in the Property inspector, change the button name to **button_home**.

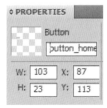

> ▶ **Tip:** Using a consistent "heading" word in each button name (such as "button_" in this exercise) makes it easier to find groups of similar graphics in Windows Explorer, the Mac Finder, or even in Dreamweaver's Files panel.

12 Click on the Our Mission button, and change the button name to **button_mission**.

13 Click on the Funding Options button, and change the button name to **button_funding**.

14 On the subsequent three buttons, change the names to **button_events**, **button_contact**, and **button_gallery**, respectively.

Testing rollovers

Now it's time to test the rollovers.

1 Click the Hide Slices And Hotspots icon ([■]) in the Tools panel.

2 Click the Preview button at the top of the document window.

3 Move your mouse over the six buttons. On each one, the gradient reverses and the text turns white when you mouse over it.

4 Switch back to Original view.

Completing the design

For a finishing touch on your mockup, you will add some text next to the top logo instance.

1   Select the Text tool.

2   In the Property inspector, choose a conservative serif font. We chose Baskerville Old Face.

3   Set the font size to 28 point. This may need some adjustment, depending on your own font selection.

4   Set the font style to Bold.

5   Click to the right of the logo at the top of the page, and type **The Bare Tree Society**. Use the Return or Enter key to break the text into three lines.

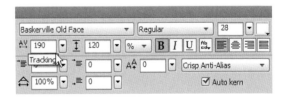

6   Select the word Society using the Text tool.

7   Change the Tracking value in the Property inspector so that the letters space out to a width matching the space used by Bare Tree. In this example, the tracking value was set to 190%.

8   Save the file.

With your main page mockup completed, save the file as **simple_page_complete** if you wish. You will not need the final version for any other lessons. You can compare your version to our completed one, simple_page_final.png, if you like.

The States panel

The States panel gives you the ability to create simple rollover effects and animations. States can also be used to represent more complex interaction, such as how a software application would look after a button was pressed.

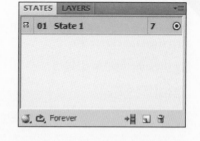

Animation symbols also make use of the States panel. Each state contains a different rendition of the animated object. This could be a change in size, location, opacity, or rotation.

By default, each new Fireworks document or page begins with a single state.

● **Note:** Prior to Fireworks CS3, the States panel was known as the Frames palette.

Animation symbols

Animation symbols let you quickly generate various types of state-based animation, including movement, visibility, opacity, and size. Because animations require multiple states in a document, they are best created on their own—either in a new document or on a separate page of an existing document, rather than as part of a complete web page design. This eliminates the potential for exporting unwanted images from other parts of the design.

Creating animation symbols

● **Note:** The animation capabilities for Fireworks are pretty basic and are suitable for creating simple GIF animations. If you are interested in creating complex animations for the Web, take the time to investigate Adobe Flash.

In your sample design, you have a small version of the logo placed at the bottom left of the page. You are going to animate this instance it so it enters the page on the left and slides over to the right, reducing in size slightly as it moves across the page. You will do this on a new page of your existing simple_page.png file.

1   Open the Pages panel by clicking on the Pages tab in the panel dock.

By default, the Pages panel is grouped with the States and Layers panels. If you cannot find the Pages panel, choose Window > Pages.

2 Create a new empty page by choosing the Options menu button (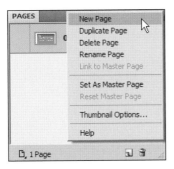) and selecting New Page.

A new, empty page is created, using the same dimensions as the original page. In the pages panel, you will now see Page 1 and Page 2.

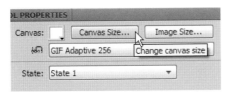

3 Change the canvas size of this page to 760 x 140 by clicking the Canvas Size button in the Property inspector. Be sure to check Current Page Only.

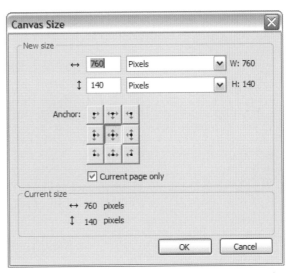

4 In the Property inspector, change the Canvas Color to #00CC00.

5 Open the Document Library panel.

6 Drag the baretree_logo symbol from the Document Library onto the canvas.

7 Scale the logo so it is 102 pixels wide by 99 pixels high, and position it at X: 16 and Y: 20.

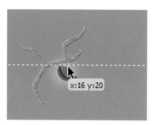

8 Right-click (Windows) or Control-click (Mac) on the symbol, and choose Animation > Animate Selection.

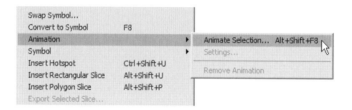

9 Change the following values in the Animate dialog box:

- States (Windows) or Frames (Mac): 9

- Move: 650

- Scale: 70

Leave all other fields as they are, and click OK.

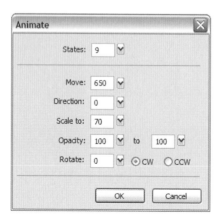

10 A dialog box appears, asking if you want to add additional states to this page. Click OK.

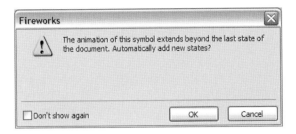

You are returned to the canvas. The logo now has a blue path attached to it, with nine anchor points, representing the nine states of the animation. The starting anchor point is green, and the ending anchor point is red.

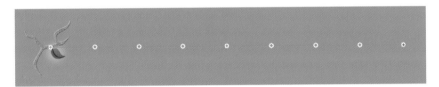

Notice that Fireworks has added this instance of the logo as a new symbol in the Document Library panel. It needs a better name.

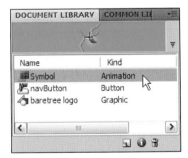

11 Double-click on the symbol in the Document Library panel to open the Convert To Symbol dialog box, and rename the symbol **logo animation**.

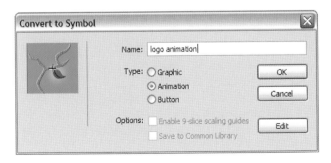

● **Note:** Any object
can be turned into an
animation symbol in
the manner described
here. You don't have to
start with a symbol.

12 Click OK.

At the bottom of the document window are animation playback controls.

13 Click the Play icon to see the animation.

● **Note:** You have also created a nested symbol by making this animation. Double-clicking the animation instance will bring you to the logo animation symbol. Double-clicking again will bring you to the original bare tree logo symbol. Any changes you make to the nested bare tree logo will update all instances of the symbol on all pages, whether they are part of the animation symbol or not. To eliminate this potential problem, you can right-click (or Control-click) the nested baretree logo symbol and choose Symbol > Break Apart. This will break the link between the artwork in the animation symbol and the original bare tree logo.

Onion skinning

Animation symbols are a bit different from just having objects in different states. The animation direction and distance is controlled by dragging the animation path in State 1. Normally, you see only the objects that are part of a selected state. However, you can use a feature called onion skinning to see as many states as you like. Onion skinning allows you to see states that occur before and after the currently selected state.

You are going to adjust the angle of the animation slightly, so the final state is at the same distance from the bottom of the screen as the first state.

1 Making sure rulers are visible (View > Rulers), drag down a guide from the top ruler so it rests at the bottom of the logo.

2 Select the logo on the canvas.

3 If necessary, open the States panel.

4 Choose Show All States from the Onion Skinning ( ) menu at the bottom of the panel.

The canvas now displays each state of the animation.

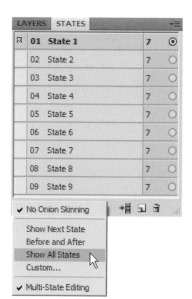

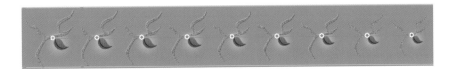

You will also notice a vertical line with start and stop nodes, running down the States panel to the left of the state names. This is a visual representation of the onion skinning. You can adjust the onion skinning settings by clicking in the onion skinning box next to each state name.

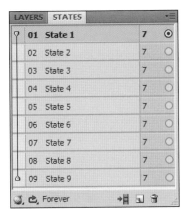

5 Click the onion skinning box next to State 5. All subsequent states disappear from the canvas.

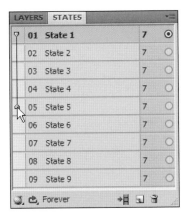

6 Click the onion skinning box next to State 9 again, to return things to how they were.

7 Select the Pointer tool.

8 Click outside the canvas area to show your canvas settings in the Property inspector.

9 Change the Canvas color to white. This will make the next steps easier.

10 Select the first state of the animation. The animation path will reappear.

You need to adjust the animation path so the states line up at the bottom edge, and you will also need to reposition the final state so it is completely within the canvas.

11 Click and drag the red anchor point lower and inward to the left, so that the last state of the animation rests on the guide you added earlier in the exercise. There is no preview for this process, nor do tooltips or guide snapping work. This will be a bit of trial and error.

12 Click outside the canvas area and then reset the canvas color to #00CC00.

Optimizing the animation

In order to make this series of states into a true web animation, you must change the format to Animated GIF. First, however, you will trim the canvas to get rid of any unnecessary image data.

1 Choose Modify > Canvas > Trim Canvas. This deletes any excess canvas area from the page.

2 Open the Optimize panel.

3 Choose Animated GIF from the Export File Format menu.

4 Set the number of colors to 256.

5 Set Transparency to Alpha Transparency. This will force the number of colors to 255, because the canvas color is now reserved as a transparent color.

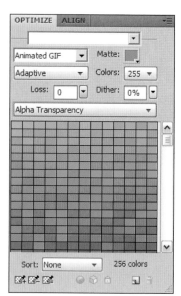

6 Set Matte color to #00CC00. The matte color helps blend the edges of an anti-aliased bitmap with the background color of the web page. If the Optimize panel says Rebuild, then click that button to rebuild the color table in the document.

7 Click the 2-Up preview button at the top of the document window.

The first thing you might notice is the glow behind the leaf is no longer a subtle gradation. As mentioned in Lesson 8, GIF images support only up to 256 colors. Typically, gradients contain a greater range of hues/tones than that, and this logo is no exception. If you compare the original view to the optimized preview, you will see the gradient in the optimized version is made up of a series of color circles. This "banding" is a result of the GIF's inability to display the full hue range of the gradient.

You will also notice the checkerboard canvas area. This checkerboard indicates a transparent area. By choosing Alpha Transparency in the Optimize panel, Fireworks will export this animated GIF with a see-through canvas area. It also saves us a few bytes in file size.

As for the banding issue, your options are to accept this result, switch to a solid-color glow, or experiment with the optimization settings. The current file size of the GIF image is approximately 20 kb. Ideally, we want to keep the file size no larger than this, but we also want a better-looking gradient.

8   Change the dither setting to 100%, and compare the images again. A higher dithering percentage creates the appearance of more colors in an image, but can also increase the file size.

9   Again, if a button labeled Rebuild appears in the Optimize panel, click it to rebuild the color table for the document.

The gradient looks only slightly better now, but this file has increased in size to about 24 kb.

Again, you need to walk the balance between image quality and file size. The process of optimization has already been explained in great detail in Lesson 8, so in this case we will simply make suggestions here. As always, you are welcome to experiment further.

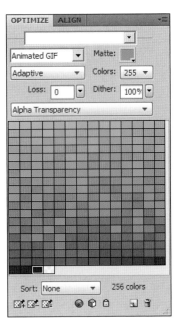

10 Change the number of colors to **32**. There is a noticeable drop in file size. And, odd as it may seem, the glow seems to have slightly less banding in it.

Now, 32 colors isn't bad, but you should be able to squeeze a bit more out of this file. Time to split some hairs. Aside from the preset color settings, you can also type in your own value for the number of colors.

11 In the Optimize panel, select number 32, and type in **28**. This gives us a file size of about 14 kb. The banding is even less noticeable. The reason for this is that due to the reduced number of colors, the dithering is being applied more heavily. Overall image quality has also been somewhat reduced, but as this will be an animation, the change should not be too noticeable.

12 Switch back to the Original view by clicking the Original button.

13 Save the file.

Other ways to reduce file size

You can reduce the file size of a GIF animation in a few different ways:

- Reduce the number of colors used, as demonstrated earlier.
- Reduce the dimensions of the animation.
- Remove states from an animation. The number of states in a GIF animation plays a big role in the final file size. By reducing the number of states to the barest minimum needed, you can significantly reduce the final file size.
- As with objects or layers, to delete a state, simply drag it to the Delete State button in the States panel.

Altering animation settings

While you can use the playback controls to watch the animation, they do not emulate the true speed of the animation. For this, you will have to preview the animation in a web browser or in the Preview window.

The speed at which the animation runs is referred to as "state delay," and by default, each state in an animation remains visible for 7/100 of a second. Increasing this value (to 20/100s, for example) will slow the animation; conversely, decreasing the value will speed up the animation. You can change the state delay for any individually selected state, or you can select a series of states and alter the delay for all of them.

1 Click the Preview button at the top of the document window.

2 Click the Play icon in the playback controls at the bottom of the document window. Click the Stop icon once the animation has run a couple of times.

3 If necessary, open the States panel.

4 In the States panel, click State 1.

5 Hold the Shift key, and then click State 9.

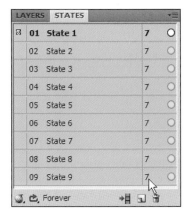

6 Double-click on any of the number 7s which appear to the right of a state name. The State properties box appears.

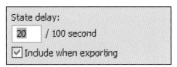

7 Change the value to **20**, and press Enter or Return. All the states are now set to 20/100 of a second.

8 Click the Play icon again. The animation plays at a much slower pace.

9 Select all the states again, change the delay to 4/100, and press Enter or Return.

10 Click the Play icon again. The animation plays much faster.

11 Reset the delay value to 7.

You can also preview the animation in a web browser by choosing File > Preview In Browser and selecting your preferred web browser. Your playback experience may vary between the browser and the Preview window in Fireworks; as with any web-destined artwork, you should always view your work in as many browsers as you have available.

Looping controls how many times an animation repeats. The default looping value is Forever. That may be useful for some generic animated graphics, but it can also be quite annoying visually.

Note: Regardless of the looping setting you choose, Fireworks will always loop the animation when you click the Play icon. To test looping, you will have to preview in a browser.

12 In the States panel, click the Looping icon ( ), and change the value from Forever to No Looping. This forces the exported animation to run once only, and stop.

13 Save the file one more time.

Note: Animated GIFs don't have a lot of features when it comes to animation, which is why you don't see a lot of fancy special options for animation in Fireworks. If you are interested in creating complex animations for the web, it would be a good idea for you to investigate Adobe Flash.

Exporting the animation

You're now ready to export the file as an animated GIF.

1 Choose File > Export.

2 Browse to the Lesson09 folder.

3 Change the name to **logo_animation.**

4 Choose Images Only for the Export type.

5 Set Slices to None, if necessary.

The Include Areas Without Slices and Current Page Only options should be selected. Because this is an animation, Current State Only should be deselected.

6 Click Save (Windows) or Export (Mac). Feel free to launch a browser and open the GIF animation from the browser's File menu or drag the file onto the page of an already open browser.

Review questions

1 What are the three main types of symbols?

2 What objects can be included in a symbol?

3 How do you create a graphic symbol?

4 What is the States panel?

5 What is the importance of the Common Library?

Review answers

1 The three main types of symbols are graphic symbols, button symbols, and animation symbols.

2 A symbol can include vector, bitmap, or text objects. You can even include other symbols in a symbol, which is referred to *nesting symbols*.

3 To create a graphic symbol, select the objects you wish to be part of the symbol, and then choose Modify > Symbol > Convert To Symbol. Name the symbol in the Convert To Symbol dialog box, and set Type to Graphic. Based on your requirements for this symbol, you can choose to select the Enable 9-slice Scaling and Save To Common Library options.

4 The States panel gives you the ability to create simple rollover effects and animations. States can also be used to represent more complex interaction, such as how a software application would look after a button was pressed. In an animation sequence, each state contains a different rendition of the animated object. This could be a change in size, location, opacity, or rotation.

5 The Common Library contains a large number of prebuilt graphic, button, animation, and component symbols that you can easily drag and drop into your design. You can also save your own custom symbols to the Common Library, so they can be used in any of your documents.

10 PROTOTYPING BASICS

Lesson overview

Fireworks is a graphical, rapid-prototyping tool with a multitude of features, including multiple pages, interactive web layers, and component symbols. Layout features (smart guides and tooltips) and the ability to switch seamlessly from vector to bitmap graphic editing make Fireworks an ideal application for building prototypes to test user interaction and nail down interface or page-design issues.

In this lesson, you'll learn how to do the following:

- Create a multipage mockup

- Share layers to multiple pages

- Use the Hotspot tool to create interactivity between pages

- Preview a mockup design in a web browser

- Export a secure, interactive PDF file

 This lesson will take about 60 minutes to complete. Copy the Lesson10 folder into the Lessons folder that you created on your hard drive for these projects (or create it now), if you haven't already done so. As you work on this lesson, you won't preserve the start files. If you need to restore the start files, copy them from the *Adobe Fireworks CS4 Classroom in a Book* CD.

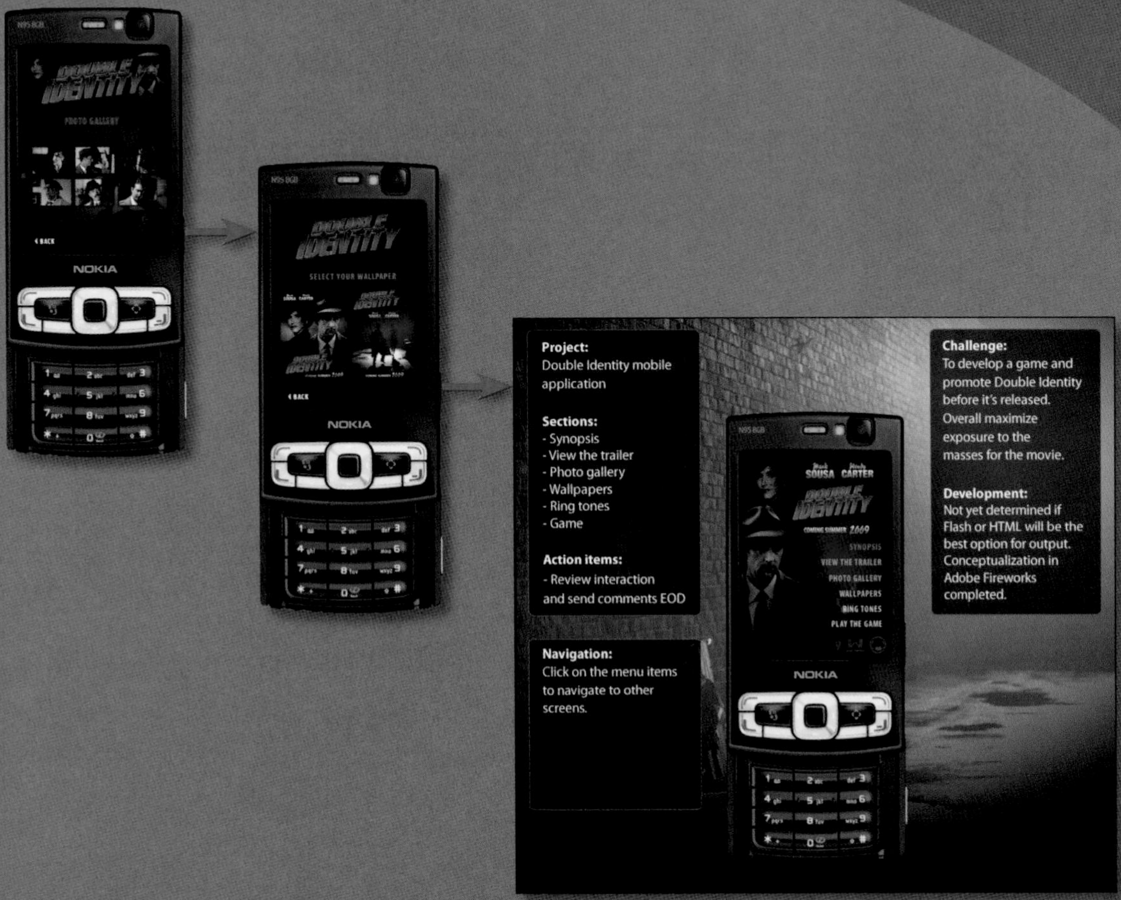
PHOTO GALLERY
BACK
NOKIA
SELECT YOUR WALLPAPER
BACK
NOKIA
Project:
Double Identity mobile application
Sections:
- Synopsis
- View the trailer
- Photo gallery
- Wallpapers
- Ring tones
- Game
Action items:
- Review interaction and send comments EOD
Navigation:
Click on the menu items to navigate to other screens.
SOUSA CARTER
SYNOPSIS
VIEW THE TRAILER
PHOTO GALLERY
WALLPAPERS
RING TONES
PLAY THE GAME
NOKIA
Challenge:
To develop a game and promote Double Identity before it's released. Overall maximize exposure to the masses for the movie.
Development:
Not yet determined if Flash or HTML will be the best option for output. Conceptualization in Adobe Fireworks completed.

Fireworks is a graphical, rapid-prototyping tool with a multitude of features, such as Pages, Interactive Web layers and Component Symbols, making it an ideal application for building prototypes to test user interaction and nail down interface or page design issues.

Exploring the Pages panel

A key prototyping strength in Fireworks is the ability to create multiple pages in a single Fireworks file. With multiple pages, you can easily generate a series of design concepts, an entire website mockup, or an application design in one location, making it easier to keep track of assets for a specific project.

And the Pages panel is the control center for adding, duplicating, deleting, and renaming pages.

To get started, you'll open the completed concept file, in order to explore the features of the Pages panel. The Pages panel is the control center for adding, duplicating, deleting, and renaming pages.

Options menu

Show/Hide Master Page Thumbnail

PAGES

background [Master Page]

01 home

02 synopsis

03 view_trailer

04 photo_gallery

05 wallpaper

06 ring_tones

07 ring_tones_1

08 ring_tones_2

09 ring_tones_3

10 crane_game

Page selector — 10 Pages

Delete page

Total page count

New/Duplicate page

Each page in a document has a sequence number automatically applied by Fireworks. This sequence number cannot be manually altered. However, you can rename any page by double-clicking on the page name, just as you can with layers and objects. If your design uses a master page for common page elements, that master page will appear at the top of the Pages panel.

Isolating the Pages panel

Typically, the Pages panel is grouped with the Layers and States panels, but we find it more useful to put it into its own group in a customized panel group. You will do that now.

1   Choose File > Open, and browse to the mobile_film_site_final.png file.

This is the almost-complete concept pitch for a cell phone application to promote the movie *Double Identity*. This version helps to illustrate some important concepts for prototyping. Later in this lesson, you will be working on a much less complete version, to build the final concept.

2   Open the Pages panel (Window > Pages).

3   Hold down the left mouse button on the Pages tab, and reposition the cursor so that it is between any two groups.

4 When a thin blue highlight bar appears, and the panel's opacity fades, release the mouse button. The Pages panel is now in its own group.

Master pages

The master page is an optional but very useful item. Use it if you have visual elements that will be common to all pages and in the same physical location. Because each page can have different dimensions, it's best to use a master page only for elements that appear at the top of a design or share a common canvas color. If you are positive your page dimensions will not change, you can also include common background images or footer information in a master page; just bear in mind that if you shorten or lengthen a page, that information may not stay in the correct position.

Each Fireworks design can contain only a single master page.

Renaming a master page

1 Locate the master page at the top of the Pages panel.

2 Double-click on the page name.

3 Change the name to **background**.

Note that while you can change the name of the master page, the identifier—[Master Page]—cannot be removed or edited.

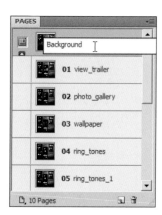

Comparing page designs

Each page in a Fireworks document can be a unique design, using different canvas dimensions, resolution, and artwork.

Each page also has its own unique Web Layer and can contain layer hierarchies, states, and graphics similar to other pages or completely different from them. This gives you a powerful advantage; you can create multiple design concepts, or a series of full-page mockups for a website, all in the same document. No more having to hunt for this file or that file for a specific client, because they are all in the same place!

1 Select the page called home by clicking on the page in the Pages panel.

2 On the canvas, zoom out enough that you can see most of the document.

3 Select the ring_tones page. Note how certain elements are exactly the same, but a lot of the visual content has changed. You'll find the same is true throughout this design.

Page stacking order

● **Note:** You can't place pages above a master page.

Page stacking order is not like layer stacking order; it is more for organization than anything else. Changing the page order does not affect what will be seen above or below a selected page, because each page is a unique design (with the exception of the Master page or shared layers). You will change the stacking order of a page to see how this renumbering works.

▶ **Tip:** Remember, to collapse a panel group, click on the dark gray bar behind the tabs.

1 Drag the bottom of the Pages panel downward to expand it. If there is not enough space on your screen to expand it, collapse other panel groups, and then try again.

2 Drag the home page to just below the synopsis page, and release the mouse. Note that the sequence number automatically updates when the page is moved.

3 Drag the home page back to its original location below the Master page.

● **Note:** Page names become HTML filenames when you export as HTML and Images or CSS and Images, so it's a good idea to follow standard naming conventions for page names, just like you would with slice names. Avoid spaces and special characters, and to keep things really simple, only use lowercase letters.

4 Save and close this file.

Creating a page for a multipage mockup

Enough of working with the finished file; you're here to learn how to build something like this, not just tweak it!

Copying a page

For this exercise, you'll open up an earlier version of the file, in which we've created a few pages for you. Most of the pages have some artwork on them, but there are many things missing. For example, the only page that has the background elements present is the home page. Click on the others and you will see there's not much there to flesh out the design. You'll copy the home page to create a new page with the background elements.

Planning the plan

Even though you are creating a mockup and are essentially still in the planning stages, it's a good idea to take some time and plan out the contents of your overall design before jumping right into Fireworks. An hour with pencil and paper can be time well spent if you are able to sketch out—in words or simple drawings—the contents of your prototype and the different pages you need to include. This process gives you focus, and is something you can refer back to as you build the skeleton of the prototype.

1   Open mobile_film_site_start.png from the Lesson10 folder.

2   In the Pages panel, drag the home page to the New/Duplicate page button. Instant new page!

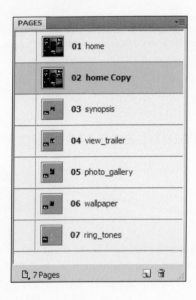

Creating a master page

Copying pages is a real time-saver! No tedious copying and pasting of objects into a new file. However, this method produces copies of *everything* from the originating page. If you only have a couple of pages in your mockup, this may not be a problem. But imagine if you had 5 or 10—or more—pages in your mockup, all generated from one original page design. Now imagine having to edit or update multiple elements—change the background image, update common text, or maybe even swap one phone model for another. Now you've got a lot more work on your hands—multiplied by the number of pages in your design.

You can improve your workflow enormously by placing common background elements on a master page. Remember, these should be objects that are going to appear on every page of your mockup, in the same X and Y positions. With our current example, there are several elements that can be appropriately added to a master page. And that is what you will do right now.

That duplicate of the home page is going to come in handy, because a master page needs to be created from an existing page.

1   Select the home Copy page in the Pages panel.

2   In the Layers panel, drag the home layer to the Delete Selection (trash can) icon. This is going to become our master page, so anything that won't be common to all the pages needs to be removed.

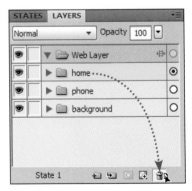

3 Select the original home page.

4 In the Layers panel, drag the phone layer to the Delete Selection (trash can) icon. You're removing this layer because its contents will be handled by the master page.

5 Delete the background layer.

Your home page should now look like all the other pages—a little bit of content on top of a gray canvas.

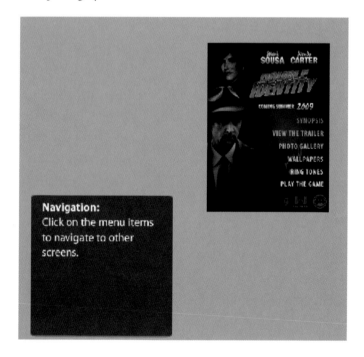

6 Select the home Copy page again.

7 Right-click (Windows) or Control-click (Mac) on the page name in the Pages panel, and choose Set As Master Page.

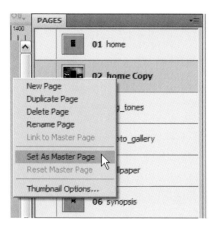

This duplicated page moves to the top of the Pages panel, and each of the existing page thumbnails refreshes with all the master page elements.

8 Select the master page (if it is not already selected), and double-click on the page name.

9 Change the name to **background**.

10 Save the file as **mobile_film_site_working.png**.

Adding more pages

There are a few pages missing from this mockup. You will add those now, using two different methods: creating a new page based on the master page, and copying pages.

1 Select the ring_tones page.

2 Click the New/Duplicate page icon at the bottom of the Pages panel.

● **Note:** New pages always appear below the currently active page.

3 A new page is created, using the attributes from the master page.

4 Rename this page **crane_game**.

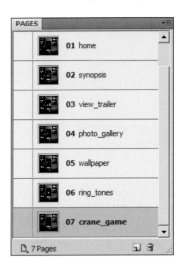

5 Make sure the rulers and tooltips are visible and Snap To Guides is active (View > Rulers, View > Tooltips, View > Guides > Snap To Guides).

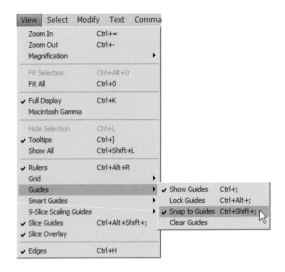

6 Drag a vertical guide from the left side ruler to a position of 365 pixels.

▶ **Tip:** If you can't seem to get the guide to stay at 365 pixels, release it and choose the Pointer tool. Move your cursor over the guide, and when you see the double-headed arrow (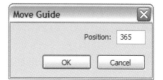), double-click on the guide. The Move Guide dialog box appears, and you can numerically set the location of the guide.

7 Drag a horizontal guide from the top ruler, and drop it at 212 pixels.

8 Switch to the Layers panel, if necessary, and rename Layer 1 to **crane_game**.

9 Choose File > Import, select the crane_game.png file in the Lesson10 folder, and click Open.

10 Position the import cursor at the intersection of the two guides.

11 Click once to import the file at its original size.

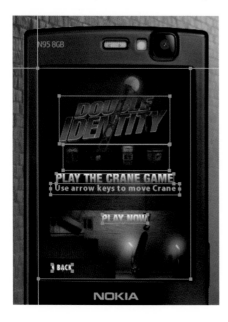

12 Save the file.

13 Select the ring_tones page in the Pages panel.

14 Drag this page to the New/Duplicate Page icon three times, for a total of four identical pages. Because the originating page was based on the master page, these new copies will also contain the master-page content.

15 Double-click on the copy directly below the original ring_tones page.

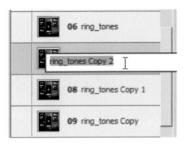

16 Rename this page **ring_tones_1**.

17 Rename the next two pages **ring_tones_2** and **ring_tones_3**, in that order.

These three extra pages will eventually display changes in the ringtone text highlights.

18 Save your work.

Sharing layers to pages

A master page is great if you want the same elements on every page, but what if you have some elements that appear on certain pages only? You could, of course, just copy and paste those elements to each page, but a little foresight (coupled with what you're about to learn) could save you a lot of time. In this exercise, you will share an existing layer with specific pages in the mockup.

1   Select the view_trailer page. This page has the movie title in the cell phone screen. You want to use this image on other pages as well.

2   In the Layers panel, select the header layer.

3   Choose Share Layer To Pages from the Layers panel menu ().

4   With the exceptions of the home and crane_game pages, add all the other pages to the Include Layer To Page(s) column.

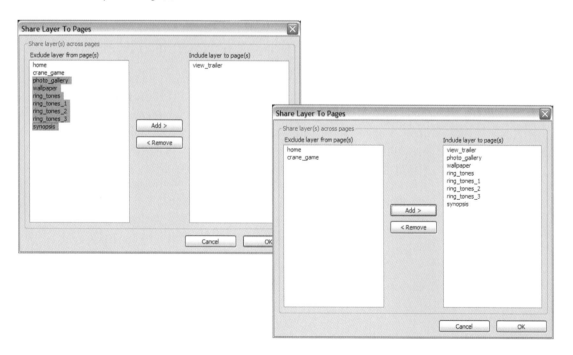

5 Click OK.

6 Select the photo_gallery page, and you'll see that the movie title now displays, as it will for the other pages sharing the header layer.

7 Save the file.

Adding hotspots for interactivity

Now that you have all your pages created, it's time to add some interactivity. Because this concept/prototype is intended for PDF distribution, you do not need to use slices in the file; PDF does not support rollover effects or state changes, and those would be the main reasons to add slicing to a document. This is also the reason you created those ring-tone duplicate pages. In a web document, you can show a state change by swapping an image on one state with an image on another state. Because PDFs can't do image-swapping, you must use pages to show state changes. Hotspots are the answer for adding interactivity to this file. You will be getting a lot of practice adding hotspots throughout this lesson, starting now.

Creating hotspots

1   Select the home page.

2   Zoom in to 200%, and reposition the document so that you can see all of the menu items in the cell phone screen.

3   Choose the Rectangle Hotspot tool ( ) from the Tools panel.

4   Draw a rectangle over the word SYNOPSIS.

5 In the Property inspector, from the Link menu, choose synopsis.htm from the list *below* the divider. The links below the divider are in your current document; links above the divider are a history list, and may be from other documents you've worked on in Fireworks in the same session.

● **Note:** Always choose your links from the list **below** the divider. These links are for the current document. If you have been working on other documents, Fireworks will maintain a history of any links selected during your current session. This list appears above the divider in the Link menu. Selecting pages from this history list will not create proper, functional links.

6 Press Enter or Return to lock in this change. This step is key to ensuring the link sticks to the hotspot.

7 Select the Pointer tool, and return to the newly made hotspot on the canvas.

8 Hold down the Alt (Windows) or Option (Mac) key and drag the hotspot to the next menu item, VIEW THE TRAILER. This creates a duplicate of the hotspot object.

▶ **Tip:** You can also use the Property inspector to change the hotspot dimensions and location.

9 Using the Pointer tool, drag a blue control point to change the width of the hotspot so it covers the entire menu item.

10 Choose view_trailer.htm from the Link menu, from the list *below* the divider in the Property inspector, and press Enter or Return to lock in the link.

11 Hold down the Alt/Option key, and drag the hotspot to the next menu item, PHOTO GALLERY.

12 Using the Pointer tool, drag a blue control point to change the width of the hotspot so it covers just the menu item.

13 Choose photo_gallery.htm from the Link menu in the Property inspector, and press Enter or Return to lock in the link.

14 Repeat this process (steps 11–13) for each of the menu items. Remember to change the link to the correct page and to press Enter or Return after selecting the link.

15 Open the Web Layer, if it is not already expanded. You now have six hotspots, all named Hotspot.

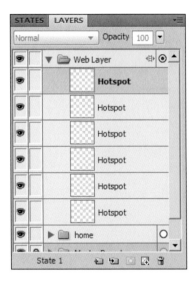

16 Select the topmost hotspot.

17 Locate the active hotspot on the canvas. Because objects are added from the bottom up, the active hotspot on the canvas will most likely be the bottom link. You will see the hotspot highlighted with the blue border and corner control points.

18 Rename the hotspot based on the page the link would point to, **crane_game**, for example.

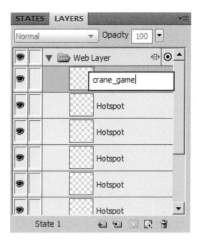

19 Rename the other five hotspots, and save your work.

When you are done, the cell phone screen area should be similar to this figure.

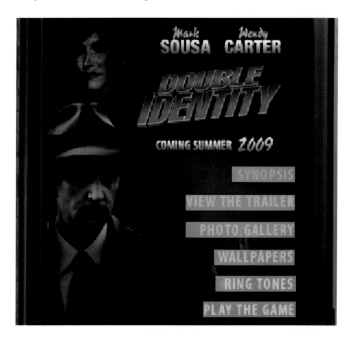

Sharing interactive objects

If you have common navigational elements, they, too, can be shared across multiple pages. This is another way you can streamline your workflow, because if you need to update a hotspot that's used on several pages, you need only change the attributes once, and all sharing pages are updated. There is a trick to this, however; interactive elements you wish to share must be placed in their own *web sublayer*. The main Web Layer cannot be shared or deleted, but you have the ability to create sublayers for web elements, just like you do for standard graphic layers.

Creating a shared a Web Layer

The cell phone image is on every page, but the Back button is not. You will have to create a web sublayer to share this interactivity to specific pages.

1 Select the synopsis page.

   Note the instructions to the client at the bottom-left of the page design—navigate back to the home screen by clicking the Back button or the upper-left cell phone button.

2 Select the Web Layer of the synopsis page.

3 Expand the Web Layer.

   It's currently empty, but you will add a sublayer.

4 Click the New Sub Layer icon at the bottom of the Layers panel.

5 Rename this new web sublayer **common_nav**.

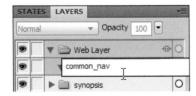

6   On the canvas, draw a rectangular hotspot over the word BACK on the cell phone.

7   Set the link in the Property inspector to home.htm, and press Enter or Return.

8   In the Layers panel menu, choose Share Layer To Pages.

9   Add all the pages except the home page to the Include Layer To Page(s) column.

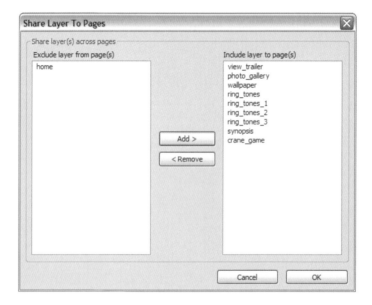

10 Click OK.

11 Rename the hotspot to **back**.

12 Click on each page. The hotspot is present and in exactly the same location on all but the home page.

Adding interactivity to the master page

The phone image is on every page, so rather than share a layer, you can add the hotspot to the Web Layer of the master page.

1 Select the master page, currently named background.

2 Select the Rectangle Hotspot tool, and draw a box over the top part of the upper-left cell phone button.

● **Note:** While it may be tempting to use the Polygon Hotspot tool to create an exact outline of the button, Acrobat recognizes only rectangular interactive objects. A polygon hotspot would be ignored in a PDF.

3 Set the link to home.htm (remember, use only the links below the divider in the Link menu) and press Enter or Return.

4 Switch to the home page.

5 Save the file.

Testing the links

Even though the end use for this concept is a PDF, it's a good idea to use the Preview In Browser feature to test the hotspot links.

1 Choose File > Preview In Browser > Preview All Pages In [primary browser].

2 When the page loads in your browser, test the link areas by clicking on them.

Emulating state changes

To show the client what happens visually when a user chooses a ringtone, you need to make some changes to the ring_tones_1, _2 and _3 pages.

1   Select the ring_tones_1 page, and make sure the ringtones layer is selected.

2   With the Pointer tool, click on the background image to deselect everything.

3   With the Text tool, set the following text properties in the Property inspector:

*   Font Family: Myriad Pro
*   Font Style: Bold Condensed
*   Size: 12 points
*   Color: White (#FFFFFF)
*   A/V (tracking): 70
*   Alignment: Left aligned
*   Stroke color: None
*   Anti-Aliasing: Smooth Anti-Alias

You can leave all other properties at their default settings. If you do not have Myriad Pro in your font collection, try Arial Narrow, Bold, at 11 points. You may need to adjust the horizontal scale to a lower value and the tracking to a higher value. Failing that, select a similar sans-serif font from your collection.

4   Click on the right side of the phone's screen, and type **DOWNLOAD.**

5   Use the Pointer tool to reposition the text block to X: 530, Y: 506. It should align with the bottom of the BACK text, positioned near the right edge of the screen.

6 Copy the text block.

7 Select the ring_tones_2 page.

8 Paste the text. It will appear in the same location.

9 Select the ring_tones_3 page, and paste the text again.

10 Deselect the DOWNLOAD text.

11 While you are still on the ring_tones_3 page, press Shift, and select the ringtone 3 heading and the song title.

12 Change the text color to **#5FB9C9**.

13 Switch to the ring_tones_2 page, and change the text color of the second ringtone heading and song title, as in step 12.

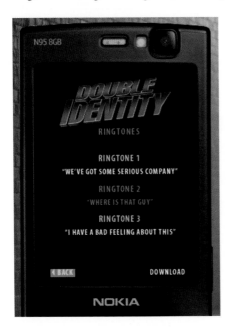

14 Repeat these steps for the ring_tones_1 page.

15 Save the file.

More hotspots!

Our last steps before exporting as a PDF will be to add interactivity to the ringtone pages.

1   Select the ring_tones page.

2   Expand the Web Layer, and make sure the Web Layer itself (not the shared common_nav layer) is highlighted. When in doubt, click once on the main Web Layer.

3   With the Rectangle Hotspot tool, draw a rectangle around the bottom of the main navigation button of the phone.

4   Choose ring_tones_1.htm from the Link menu in the Property inspector. Press Enter or Return to lock in the link change.

5   In the Layers panel, rename the hotspot to **ringtones1**.

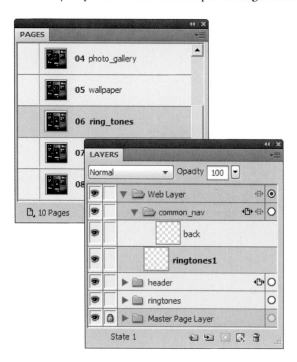

6   Switch to the ring_tones_1 page.

7   Expand the Web Layer, and make sure the Web Layer itself (not the shared common_nav layer) is highlighted.

8   Draw two hotspot boxes, one on top of the upper part of the button and one on the lower part.

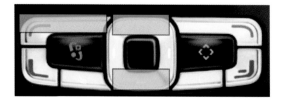

9   Select the top hotspot, and set the link to ring_tones.htm.

10 Select the lower hotspot, and set the link to ring_tones_2.htm.

11 In the Layers panel, rename the top hotspot **ringtones** and the bottom hotspot **ringtones2**.

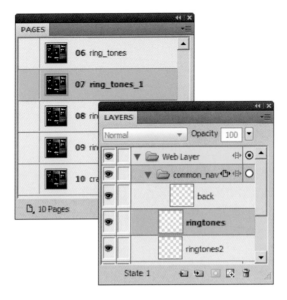

12 Select the two hotspots in the Web Layer, and choose Edit > Copy.

13 Switch to the ring_tones_2 page.

14 Expand the Web Layer, and make sure the main Web Layer itself is highlighted.

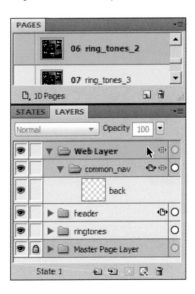

15 Choose Edit > Paste.

16 On the canvas, select the upper hotspot.

17 Change the link to ring_tones_1.htm. Remember to press Enter or Return.

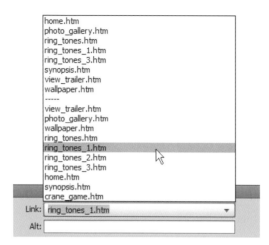

18 Select the lower hotspot.

19 Change the link to ring_tones_3.htm, and press Enter or Return.

20 Rename the hotspots accordingly in the Web Layer.

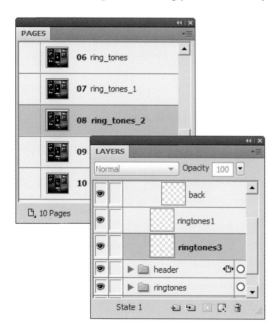

21 Switch to ring_tones_3. Repeat steps 14–20, changing the upper hotspot's link to ring_tones_2.htm and the lower hotspot's link to ring_tones.htm.

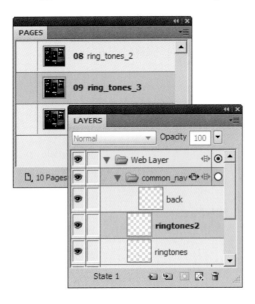

22 Save the file.

⬤ **Note:** Depending on the order in which you add the hotspots on the canvas, their stacking order in the Layers panel may not reflect their physical location on the canvas. This is not a problem, but if you find it confusing, just drag the hotspots until they represent the same vertical order as they do on the canvas. Take care not to accidentally drag the hotspot into the common_nav web layer.

Creating a secure, interactive PDF

You are finally there! All that work is about to come to fruition—in producing an interactive PDF file from your multipage Fireworks design. Although interactive PDFs are but one way to create a prototype, they can be especially helpful for presenting concepts and for offline review and commenting.

1 Choose File > Export.

2 In the Export dialog box, create a new folder in the Lesson10 folder, and call it **PDF_export**.

3 Change the filename to **mobile_film_site.pdf**.

4 Set the Export type to Adobe PDF.

5 Choose All Pages from the Pages menu. If you choose Current Page, all interactivity is disabled.

6 Make sure the View PDF After Export option is selected.

7 Click the Options button.

In the Adobe PDF Export Options dialog box, you can set many common PDF attributes such as file compatibility, image compression and quality, text selection, and security. You can set a password to protect the entire document, as well as a password to enable certain features within the PDF. You'll only change one option here.

8 Select the Use Password To Open Document option.

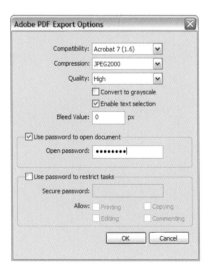

9 For this exercise, type in an easy-to-remember password, such as **fireworks**.

10 Click OK, and then click Save (Windows) or Export (Mac).

Once Fireworks exports the file, your default PDF reader will launch. If you own Acrobat Professional, you can make this PDF file even more useful by enabling the commenting feature. This will allow users to open the file in Adobe Reader®, add comments, save the file, and e-mail it back to you with their feedback.

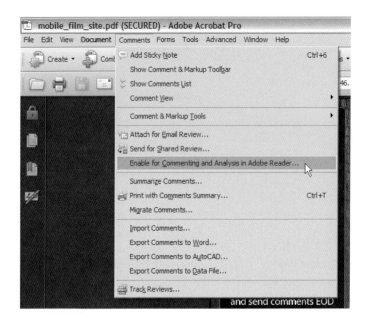

Review questions

1 What are the benefits of using a master page?

2 What are the steps for sharing a layer to other pages?

3 How do you create a copy of an existing page?

4 What type of hotspots can be used when you plan to export an interactive PDF?

5 How do you share a Web Layer?

Review answers

1 The master page can be used for displaying common elements across all pages in a design, such as a header or a background. This speeds up the creation of other pages, because all pages are initially based on the master page. When you edit an object on a master page, that edit is reflected on all pages in the design.

2 Select the layer you wish to share from the Layers panel, and choose Share Layer To Pages from the Layers panel menu. In the Share Layer To Pages dialog box, add the pages you wish to share the layer with, and click OK.

3 To create a copy of an existing page, drag the page from the Pages panel to the Add/Duplicate Page icon at the bottom of the Pages panel.

4 You can use only rectangular hotspots for creating interactive hotspots if you plan to export the file as an interactive PDF. Acrobat will ignore circular and polygonal hotspots.

5 In order to share interactive objects like hotspots, they must be placed in a web sublayer. The main Web Layer cannot be shared, deleted, or renamed, but a web sublayer can.

11 ADVANCED PROTOTYPING

Lesson overview

Fireworks gives you the power (and the tools) to create fully interactive, clickable HTML mockups. In Fireworks, it's easy to create button rollovers and emulate pop-up windows.

As you work through this lesson, remember that Fireworks is an excellent graphics editor; however, it is not designed to be, nor should you expect it to be, an HTML web page editor.

In this lesson, you'll learn how to do the following:

- Create a multipage website mockup
- Use the Slice tool to slice up graphics in a web page mockup
- Use the Slice tool to create a rollover effect
- Use the Hotspot tool to trigger a disjointed rollover (pop-up window)
- Simulate a Spry data table (disjointed rollovers)
- Preview an interactive web page design in a web browser
- Export an interactive mockup of a website

 This lesson will take about 120 minutes to complete. Copy the Lesson11 folder into the Lessons folder that you created on your hard drive for these projects (or create it now), if you haven't already done so. As you work on this lesson, you won't preserve the start files. If you need to restore the start files, copy them from the *Adobe Fireworks CS4 Classroom in a Book* CD.

Fireworks gives you the power to create a fully interactive, clickable HTML mockup using standard Fireworks tools. Creating button rollovers and emulating pop-up windows can be easily done.

Prototype orientation

Many of the concepts you learned in Lesson 10 will apply to this lesson as well, so you'll have the opportunity to practice them again. In situations where a topic was covered thoroughly in the previous lesson, we will walk you through the steps once in this lesson, but refer you back to Lesson 10 for more details.

You'll open the completed website prototype first (check_mag_site_final.png), in order to familiarize yourself with the final goals. If you are prompted about missing fonts, simply choose Maintain Appearance for now, as we will not be interacting with this file much. This is the completed web-page mockup that you will be building during this lesson.

You may recall from the last lesson that we moved the Pages panel into its own group in the panel dock—a setup we find more useful and convenient than its default location. If your Pages panel is not still in its own group, drag to position it as such now.

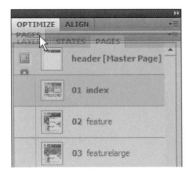

Master page

In Lesson 10, you learned that the master page is an optional item. Use it if you have visual elements that will be common to all pages and in the same physical location. In this sample file, you have common elements for the header, so it uses a master page.

1 Select the master page at the top of the Pages panel.

2 Notice that several graphics that are common to each page in the mockup are present in the master page.

Content pages

In this final mockup, all the pages have been named using standard naming conventions. This is especially important because you will be generating HTML pages from this file. You will look now at a page that includes the master-page elements as well as its own distinct graphics.

1 Select the page called index. You may recall this page from Lesson 8 ("Optimizing for the Web").

2 Zoom out enough that you can see most of the document.

3   Click Show Slices And Hotspots in the Tools panel.

There are several hotspots applied to the objects from the master page, as well as slices created specifically for this page.

4   Click on the individual slices, and note that there are a variety of file formats, each customized for the graphics below them.

The links are common to each page, so it makes sense to apply the hotspots to a shared Web Layer.

5   Open the Web Layer, and expand the web sublayer called banner nav.

The hotspots for the banner navigation reside here and are shared to all pages.

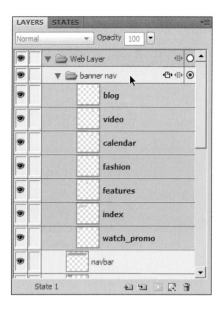

6   Close the file without saving it.

Fleshing out the prototype

To expedite the lesson, most of the art for the pages has already been added. You will, however, create two new pages—the fashion and video pages—and add the art to them. Most of your time will be spent building the interactivity for this prototype.

You had a chance in Lesson 10 to build pages for a concept. In this lesson, you will be adding two pages to the mocked-up site, and ensuring the pages are linked to the other pages in the mockup.

Creating the master page

Because this is a website mockup and pages may vary in length, only common elements that appear at the top of the page will be included in the master page.

1   Open check_mag_site_start.png. If you are prompted about missing fonts, choose Replace Fonts and select fonts on your system that have similar names or that look similar to any fonts you're missing. A quick search of the Internet for the font name will yield many results for common font names.

2   Select the header page, if it is not already active.

3   Select the index page. You'll notice that the header content is missing for the index page, and all subsequent pages.

4   Right-click (Windows) or Control-click (Mac) on the header page in the Pages panel, and choose Set As Master Page.

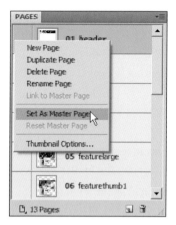

Adding more pages

1   Select the page called blog.

2   Right-click (or Control-click) on the blog page, and choose New Page.

3   Rename this page to **video**.

4   Click the Add/Duplicate Page icon.

5 Rename this page to **fashion**. You will be adding content to these pages shortly, but first you will add the main navigation and slice the header graphics.

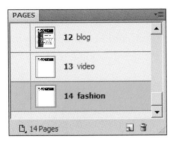

● **Reminder:** Page names become HTML filenames when you export as HTML and Images or CSS and Images, so it's a good idea to follow standard naming conventions for page names, just like you would with slice names. Avoid spaces and special characters, and, to keep things really simple, only use lowercase letters.

Slicing the banner

In order to properly export these elements for a web page, the banner area needs to be sliced.

1 Select the index page.

2 Zoom in to 200%.

3 Select the Slice tool, and draw slices around all three main banner graphics: the watch, the movie banner, and the logo/navigation bar.

4 Zoom in to at least 400% to make sure your slices properly cover each graphic. If any of your slices are not the correct dimensions, use the Pointer tool to drag the control points of the slices to set the right dimension.

5 In the Layers panel, name the watch slice **promo**.

6 Name the movie banner **feature_banner**.

7 Name the logo/navigation graphic **navbar**.

The names are kept generic enough that new images could be swapped in for web-page updates without having to rewrite filenames or update HTML.

8 In the Property inspector, set the Slice export settings for the promo and feature_banner slices to JPEG - Better Quality.

9 In the Optimize panel, set the Export file format for the navbar slice to PNG 8.

● **Note:** Because these graphics are part of the master page, you can't right-click (or Control-clcik) on the graphics to insert rectangular slices without first switching to the master page. And if the slices were created on the master page, Fireworks would try to export those slices for every page in your document, resulting in a lot of requests from Fireworks to overwrite existing files and wasting time.

Banner navigation

There are several elements within the banner area that will act as navigation for the prototype. You will add hotspots for this interactivity now.

1   Select the index page, if necessary, and select the Web Layer.

2   Choose New Sub Layer from the Layers panel menu.

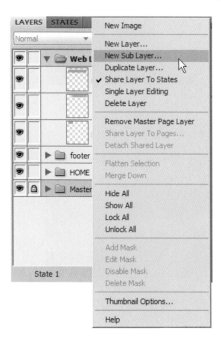

3   Name the new sublayer **banner nav**.

4   Right-click (or Control-click) on the sublayer, and choose Share Layer To All Pages from the context menu.

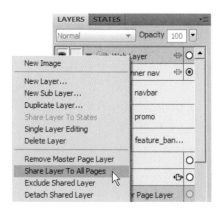

5 Select the Rectangle Hotspot tool from the Web section of the Tools panel, and draw a rectangle hotspot over the watch graphic.

6 In the Property inspector, set the link to ad_popup.htm.

7 In the Alt field, type **View the watch advertisement**.

8 Draw a new hotspot over most of the logo, Check, as seen here.

9 Set the link to index.htm.

10 In the Alt field, type **Return to home page**.

11 Draw a hotspot over each of the main navigation text objects: features, fashion, calendar, video, and blog.

● **Note:** If you prefer to input your links manually, don't forget to add *.htm* to the end of the page name.

12 Select each hotspot, one at a time, and set the link in Property inspector to the corresponding page.

13 In the Alt field, type **Link to** and add the appropriate page. For example, with the features hotspot, you would type **Link to Features page**.

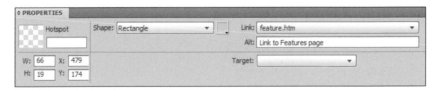

14 When you've added all the navigation hotspots, save the file as
check_mag_site_working.png.

Customizing page dimensions

The index page was based on the original page dimensions, but if you scroll down
to the bottom of the page, you'll see a lot of empty space between the text and the
footer. This white space is unnecessary, so you will shorten the length of this specific
page so the footer is closer to the text.

1 Right-click (or Control-click) on the footer layer in the Layers panel.

2 Choose Detach Shared Layer. This retains a copy of the footer on the current
page, but it is no longer linked to the original shared layer. You need to do this
in order to customize the position of the footer text on the page.

3 Select the footer text using the Pointer tool.

4 In the Property inspector, change the Y value to 940.

5 Choose Modify > Canvas > Canvas Size.

6 Set the height to 970 pixels.

7 Change the anchor point to the top middle one.

8 Select the Current Page Only option.

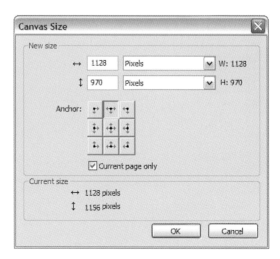

9 Click OK.

Image rollover effects

The feature page is where you really start to work! Each thumbnail on the left side needs to have a rollover effect applied to it, and also needs interactivity to link to a different mockup page. You'll create a rollover effect that changes the thumbnails from a sepia-tone image to a full image. You will be working with commands, states, slices, and shared layers for this part of the exercise. Hey, we did say this was the advanced lesson, after all!

Adding a rollover state

A rollover effect needs content on a separate state for the rollover to work. You will add the new state in this exercise.

1   Select the feature page.

2   In the Layers panel, expand the feature layer.

This layer holds all the objects that are specific to the feature pages. To further structure the file, many objects have been placed in separate sublayers. This feature layer has also been shared to other pages, as indicated by the familiar icon at the right of the layer name.

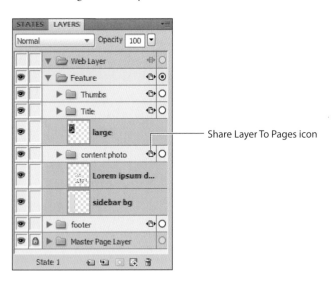

Share Layer To Pages icon

3 In the Layers panel menu, choose Share Layer To Pages.

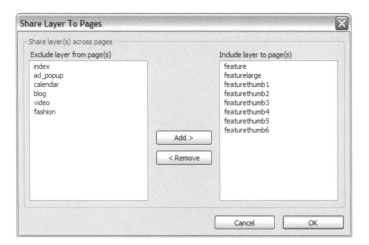

The Share Layer To Pages dialog box shows that this layer is shared to a total of eight pages. As you learned in the previous lesson, this sharing can expedite some editing tasks; as you change objects in a shared layer, those changes are propagated to all the pages that share the layer. This includes the editing, visibility, and addition/deletion of objects or sublayers within the shared layer.

The importance—and limitations— of sublayers

Sublayers are a great organizational tool; rather than having to search for individual objects within a long list of layers, you can group related objects into sublayers.

Layer and sublayer hierarchy is also preserved as layer groups when a page is saved as a Photoshop file. Similarly, if you open a Photoshop file in Fireworks that contains Photoshop layer groups, that layer hierarchy would also be preserved. Photoshop integration would seem to be a significant reason for the creation of sublayers in Fireworks.

Sublayers do have their limitations, however. When you copy a layer that contains sublayers, only the parent layer elements are copied to the clipboard; sublayers are ignored.

If you copy a sublayer, only the objects within the sublayer are copied. So if you were to paste the clipboard contents into a new design, only the objects—and not the actual sublayer that contained them—would be pasted.

If you share a layer to other pages, all sublayers are automatically shared with that page as well. You cannot selectively share certain sublayers with different pages.

4 Click Cancel to dismiss the Share Layer To Pages dialog box.

5 Expand the thumbs sublayer, and select the thumb1 object in the sublayer.

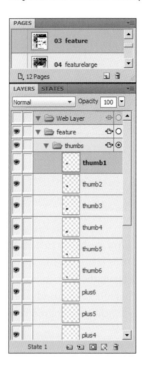

6 Scroll down in the Layers panel until you see the thumb6 object.

7 Hold down Shift, and click on the thumb6 object. This selects all six thumbnail images.

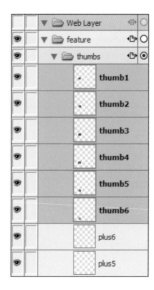

8 Choose Edit > Copy.

9 Open the States panel.

All files opened in Fireworks have at least one state—the current one. You will now add another state to the feature page.

10 Choose Add States from the States panel menu.

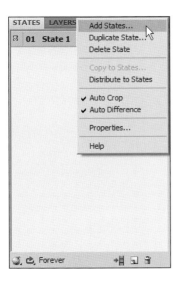

11 When the Add States dialog box appears, click OK. The defaults are fine for our simple purposes.

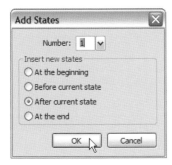

A new empty state appears in the States panel.

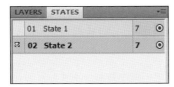

12 Go back to the Layers panel, and make sure the feature layer is still active.

13 Choose Edit > Paste. The color thumbnails appear on the new state, in exactly the same location as on the original state.

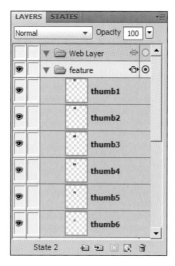

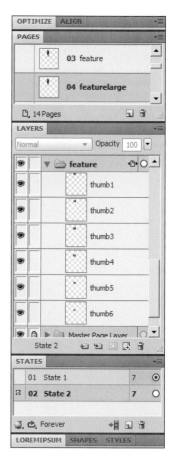

In order for the rollover to work in the mockup, the new state needs to be added to all pages.

14 Select the featurelarge page.

15 Choose Add States from the States panel menu.

16 Click OK, accepting the defaults again.

The new state appears, containing your rollover images. In this figure, we have separated the States panel from the Layers panel, so you can more easily see the relationship between the panels.

17 Repeat steps 15 and 16 for the six remaining feature pages.

Creating the rollover effect

You will make a small change to the State 1 thumbnails, so that you can establish the rollover effect.

1 Select State 1 again, in any feature page where you can easily select all six thumbnails. This is a shared layer, remember, so we can edit it from any page that it's shared to.

2 Shift-click to select each thumbnail, if they are not already selected.

3 Choose Commands > Creative > Convert To Sepia Tone.

This applies an editable Live Filter to all six images.

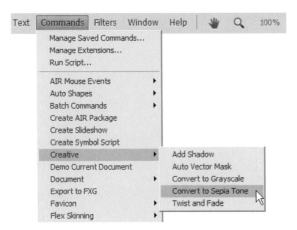

Creating the rollover slices

Now you will add the slices needed for the rollovers. Make sure all six objects are still selected.

1 Right-click (or Control-click) on any of the six thumbnails, and choose Insert Rectangular Slice from the context menu.

● **Note:** If for some reason the context menu does not give you this option, first check to make sure all the slices are selected, and then choose Edit > Insert > Rectangular Slice.

2 Choose Multiple from the alert box. You need multiple individual slices, instead of one large slice covering all six images, so that each image can have an independent rollover effect applied to its slice.

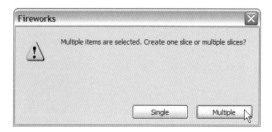

Each thumbnail now has a slice applied to it, and the slices are currently selected.

3 Choose JPEG – Better Quality from the Slice Export Settings in the Property inspector.

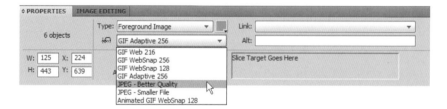

Because these rollover effects are going to be used on many pages, you should share the slices.

4 Right-click (or Control-click) on the Web Layer in the Layers panel, and choose New Sub Layer from the context menu.

5 Change the sublayer name to **thumbs**, and click OK.

6 The slices you created should still be selected. If they are not, select the top slice in the Web Layer, and then hold Shift and click the bottom slice.

7 Choose Edit > Cut.

8 Select the new thumbs web sublayer.

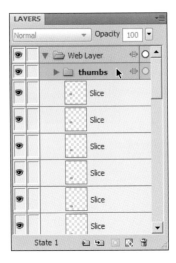

9 Choose Edit > Paste. The image slices are now part of the web sublayer.

10 Choose Share Layer To Pages from the Layers panel menu.

11 Add all the feature pages to the Include Layer(s) To Pages list, and then click OK.

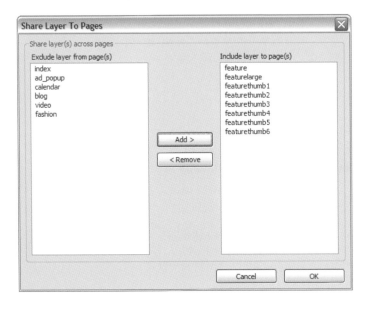

▶ **Tip:** It can be difficult to tell when objects are part of any sublayer. When in doubt, collapse the sublayer. If the objects become hidden, you know they are part of that sublayer.

Name your slices

Even though you are building a mockup here, it is entirely likely that these thumb-nails—and their rollover counterparts—will be needed for the final website. With that in mind, you will name each slice.

● **Note:** If the active slice on the canvas is not the topmost thumbnail image (which can happen, depending on the order in which the slices were added), name it accordingly. For example, if the slice is the third from the top, name it *thumb3*.

1   In the new thumbs web sublayer, select the top slice in the stack. Then, locate the active slice object on the canvas, which should be the slice that appears superimposed on the topmost thumbnail image.

2   In the thumbs web sublayer, name this slice **thumb1**. A generic, functional name is a good idea, in case the image content changes.

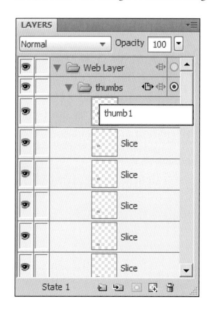

● **Note:** Because slices are usually exported, each slice name must be unique, or you run the risk of overwriting your graphics while you export them.

3   Select each of the remaining thumbnail slices, one at a time, and rename them, from top to bottom, **thumb2**, **thumb3**, **thumb4**, **thumb5**, and **thumb6**.

4   When the naming is done, save your work.

▶ **Tip:** If your slice or object names have a common element (such as thumb, in this case), save yourself some typing by selecting the text while your cursor is active in the object's label field, and then copying it. When you double-click on the next object you need to name, just paste the copied text into the field and finish off the name.

Adding rollover behaviors

Now it's time to add interactivity to these slices. But first, let's recap. You have two states for the thumbnails, each containing a different version of each thumbnail image. The feature layer is shared to all the feature pages. There is a uniquely named image slice covering each thumbnail. These slices are in a web sublayer called thumbs, and that web sublayer is shared to all the feature pages as well. Get ready to make all this work—states, thumbnail versions, slices, shared layers—come together as rollovers.

1 Make sure all six slices are selected. You will see a small circle in the middle of each slice. This is the *behavior handle*.

2 Click on the behavior handle of any of the six slices.

3 Choose Add Simple Rollover Behavior.

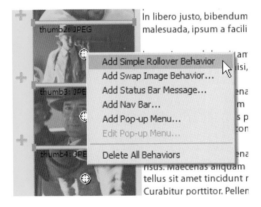

4 Save the file.

What are behaviors?

Behaviors are a quick way to add JavaScript functionality to a web page mockup, without having to write a single line of JavaScript code. Image rollovers are a pretty common use of JavaScript in web pages (although CSS-based rollover effects are becoming more popular). Behaviors are also used in Dreamweaver for creating rollover effects, navigation bar effects, and many other JavaScript-driven events.

5   Choose File > Preview In Browser > Preview In [primary browser]. In our case, the default browser is Firefox. Yours may very well be a different web browser.

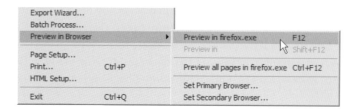

When the web browser loads the mockup, move your mouse over the thumbnails. Each image should change from a sepia-tone to a full-color image.

6   Close the browser, and return to Fireworks.

Emulating pop-up windows

Each of the large images in our design is a unique size, and the goal is to display each image as if it were popping up on top of the feature page. Having a unique slice for each different image and attempting to achieve this effect on a single page in Fireworks would be problematic, because Fireworks handles overlapping slices by generating multiple smaller slices to make up the image. The result is a lot of small images on export, with the potential for unpredictable display results.

In order to mimic a pop-up window, where the window varies in size, you can use pages to display the unique content.

Are pop-up windows evil?

The dreaded pop-up window: it's so feared that all major browsers have some form of defense against allowing it to display without the user's permission. These "pop-up blocker" mechanisms are in place because, too often, pop-up windows are either used incorrectly—windows popping up all over the desktop because they were not set up properly—or used as an intentional annoyance by some nefarious advertiser, bent on dominating the user's desktop with a myriad of ads.

But while many users consider them irritating, pop-up windows, when properly executed, can be very useful for a website. There are many things to consider when creating true pop-up windows, in order to make them accessible and searchable (two things that contribute to their usefulness). It's beyond the scope of this book to discuss those details, but you can check out sitepoint.com for a discussion on building better JavaScript pop-up windows (www.sitepoint.com/article/perfect-pop-up).

You must now add links to these six thumbnail slices.

1   Select each slice, and choose the appropriate link from the Property inspector's Link menu. For example, the thumb1 slice should link to featurethumb1.htm.

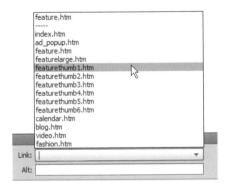

You should also add a link for the main feature image, though you won't bother with a rollover for this one.

2   Draw a hotspot over the large plus sign (+) and the word ENLARGE.

3   Set the link for this hotspot to go to featurelarge.htm.

4 Make sure the hotspot is in the thumbs web sublayer. Drag it into the sublayer, if necessary.

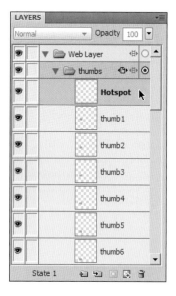

5 Rename this latest hotspot to **main_feature**.

6 When you have added all the links, save the file.

7 Choose File > Preview In Browser > Preview All Pages In [primary browser], and test the links.

Clicking on the thumbnails should take you to the proper page.

Emulating a Spry data table

Ajax (Asynchronous JavaScript and XML) gives you the ability to create dynamic web pages without forcing the entire web page to refresh. SPRY is Adobe's frame-work for Ajax, and is geared to making it easier for designers to create these dynamic elements within Dreamweaver. Granted, these definitions are very simplistic—a detailed discussion of either Spry or Ajax is not within the scope of this book—but with a little understanding of the desired end result, you can, for example, mock up the feature page like a dynamic photo gallery or data table within Fireworks. Our sample Check website requires the creation of a dynamic data area for the calendar page, and Fireworks—with your help—can create the look and feel for client feedback, before a single line of code is written.

1 Select the calendar page.

2 Open the States panel.

The calendar page has a total of seven states, each one representing a different state for the calendar menu or the detail section of the data table.

3   Click on the silver_lake state, and note how the left side of the page is updated with new content. (We've undocked the States panel so you can better see the relationship.)

4   Switch to the Layers panel. Here you can select different states by choosing from the Current State pop-up menu at the lower left of the panel.

5   Choose the up state. Note the orange-colored background behind the calendar menu.

6 Choose the over state, and note the change in the background color.

By adding in some new content, and making use of slices and behaviors, you will make this into a completely interactive page.

7 Select the up state again, and then select the main Web Layer from the Layers panel.

It is important these slices do not get added to the shared banner nav web sublayer.

8 With the Pointer tool, while holding down Shift, click on the large black and white photo and the text block on the left side of the page.

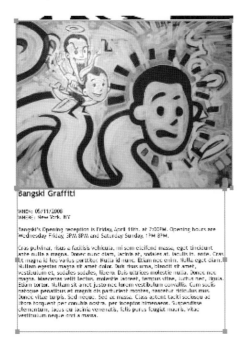

9 Right-click (or Control-click), and choose Insert Rectangular Slice.

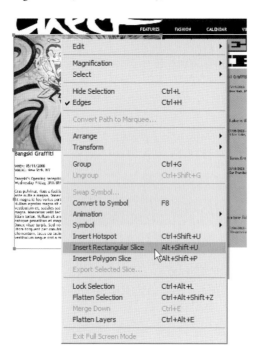

10 Click the Single button when prompted, so that the two areas are covered by a single slice. Change the Slice export settings in the Property inspector to JPEG – Better Quality.

11 Rename the slice **table_data**.

12 Change the height of the slice to 680 pixels.

13 Moving over to the calendar section on the right of the page, with the Zoom tool, draw a box over the top thumbnail and text in the calendar. You want to be able to see the background from side to side.

14 Select the Slice tool, and draw a slice that covers the orange background, thumbnail, and text for the top event. The slice should include a bit of orange background at the bottom.

15 Select the Pointer tool, hold down the Alt (Windows) or Option (Mac) key, and drag copies of the slice object over the other three calendar events. Position the slices with the help of the smart guides.

16 You'll see that the Skate event requires a larger slice than you've created, so drag the control points of the slice to set a dimension that covers the entire area. When you're done, there should be no gaps between the slices.

17 Select all four slices.

18 Change the Slice export settings in the Property inspector to JPEG – Better Quality.

Rename the four slices, from the top to the bottom, **cal_event1**, **cal_event2**, **cal_event3**, and **cal_event4**.

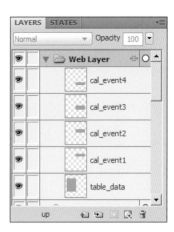

19 In the States panel, select the skater state.

20 Making sure the calendar layer is still selected, choose File > Import, and browse to the Lesson11 folder.

21 Locate and open the skater.png file.

22 When the import icon appears, place it at the upper-left corner of the table_data slice.

23 Click to import the file.

24 If the imported images do not appear exactly where you want, use the arrow keys to accurately reposition the objects so they are covered by the slice.

25 Select the architorture state, and repeat steps 20–23, importing the architorture.
png file this time.

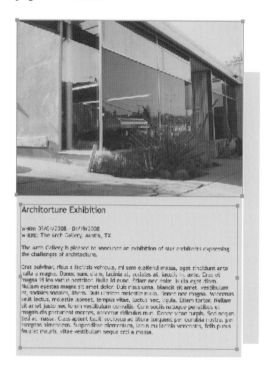

26 Save your work.

Working with behaviors

Creating this simulation is fun, and probably a lot easier than you think. You will be adding pre-built JavaScript behaviors and then editing them with the Behaviors panel.

Adding the behaviors

1 Still in the Layers panel, select the up state.

2 Use the Pointer tool to select the cal_event1 slice.

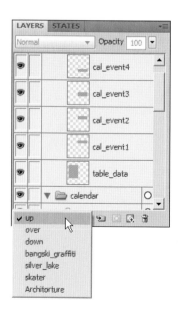

3 Click on the Behavior handle, and choose Add Navbar.

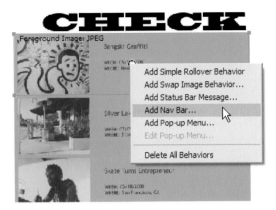

The Set Nav Bar Image dialog box gives you the chance to set other optional settings, but you will leave those options deselected.

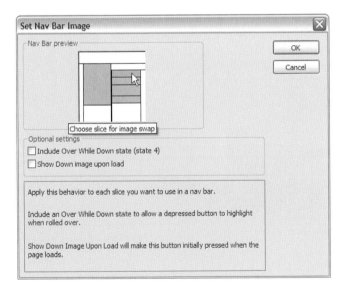

4 Click OK.

5 Use the Pointer tool to drag the behavior handle over to the table_data slice. A curved blue line will connect the slices, and a dialog box will appear.

6   Select bangski_graffiti (4) from the Swap Image From menu. This creates your
    remote image change.

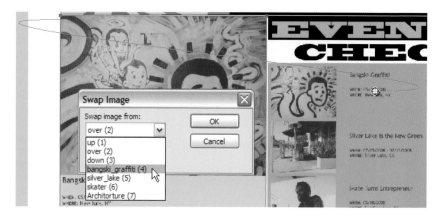

7   Click the More Options button.

8   Deselect the Restore Image OnMouseOut option. This makes the effect "sticky,"
    meaning it won't change back unless there is additional user interaction.

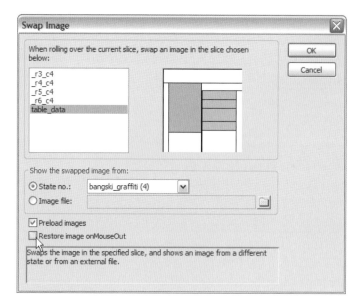

9   Click OK.

10 Repeat this process with the other event slices, making sure to select the right
    rollover for each (associating the cal_event2 slice with silver_lake (5), and so on).

Editing JavaScript behaviors

You have just created in a visual manner a series of JavaScript events. As mentioned earlier, Fireworks (and Dreamweaver) call these prebuilt events *behaviors.* Using them does not require any knowledge of JavaScript, nor do you need to edit the actual JavaScript code. However, you can customize the behaviors using the Behaviors panel.

The default event for this type of image swap is for the table_data image to change when the user's mouse moves over event slices. This is referred to as a remote, or disjointed, rollover. In your case, though, you want the appropriate table_data image to swap in when the user clicks on the matching slice, rather than when the user mouses over the area.

This is where the Behaviors panel comes to your aid.

1   Select the cal_event1 slice.

2   Choose Window > Behaviors.

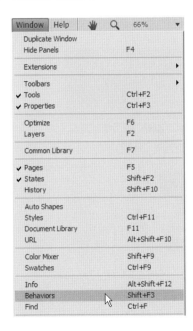

3   Select the onMouseOver event, which is part of the Swap Image action.

4   Choose onClick.

5   Select the cal_event2 slice on the canvas.

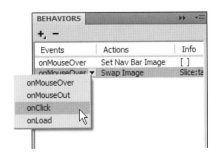

6 In the Behaviors panel, select the onMouseOver event, which is part of the Swap Image action.

7 Choose onClick.

▶ **Tip:** If the Behaviors panel is getting in the way, you can either collapse it by clicking on the Behaviors tab, or you can dock it with the other panel groups on the right side of the application.

8 Repeat the process with the other two slices, and save your work.

9 To test out our dynamic data table simulation, click the Preview button at the top of the document window.

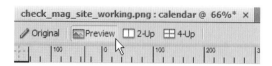

10 In the Tools panel, choose Hide Slices And Hotspots.

11 Move your mouse over the top slice. The background gets lighter. That is your swap image at work.

12 Move down to the next slice.

The silver lake event button gets brighter, and the graffiti button goes back to normal. As you move from event to event, the swapped image is restored. This is the standard mouse-over behavior people expect to see.

13 Click on the silver lake event.

The left side of the page updates with the silver_lake state, and the event remains highlighted. This information will remain until you click on another event.

14 Click on the skater event. Again, the left side updates.

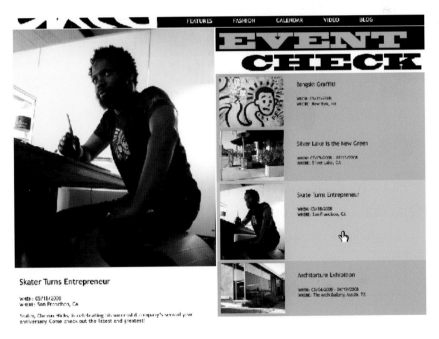

15 Switch back to the Original view, and save the file.

Completing the prototype

You have accomplished quite a bit so far—just a little more work to do before this prototype is complete.

Populating the last pages

Remember way back near the beginning of this lesson, you added two new pages—video and fashion. Well, your crowning touches on this prototype are to add the visuals for those pages.

1 Select the video page.

2 Drag a vertical guide, and place it 73 pixels in from the left.

3 Drag down a horizontal guide, and place it at 200 pixels.

   These guides will help you import the content for the video page.

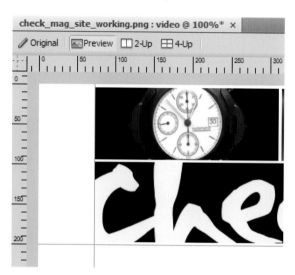

4 Choose File > Import, and browse to the Lesson11 folder.

5 Locate and open the video.png file.

6 Place the import cursor at the intersection of the two guides, and click to import.

The video content is now in place.

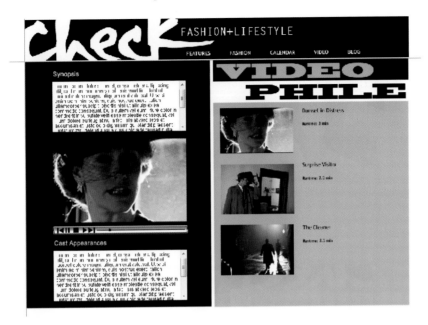

7   Switch to the fashion page, and set up guides at the same positions.

8   Import the fashion.png file.

9 Place your import cursor at the intersection of the two guides, and click to import.

10 Save your work.

Exporting the prototype

Your final step in the initial prototype is to export the design so the client can test-drive the flow and function of the site (and of course, be impressed with your graphic design skills!).

1 Choose File > Export.

2 Browse to the Lesson11 folder, and create a new folder there called **check_site**.

3 Open (Windows) or select (Mac) the new folder.

4 Choose HTML and Images from the Export list.

5 Make sure that the HTML field reads Export HTML File, and that the Slices field reads Export Slices.

6 Deselect the Current Page Only option, as you want to export all your pages for the click-through.

7 Make sure Include Areas Without Slices is selected. You sliced only a specific number of elements—mostly for interactivity purposes—and if you don't export unsliced areas, your web pages will not look right.

8 Make sure Put Images In Subfolder is selected, too, just to keeps things a bit more orderly. You can browse to an images folder in your prototype directory, or let Fireworks create a default images folder for you.

> ● **Note:** The Choose HTML and Images option generates a series of table-based HTML pages, which are fine for prototype testing, but due to the vast number of images and the rigid table structure of the pages, this export is not recommended for use as the final production website.

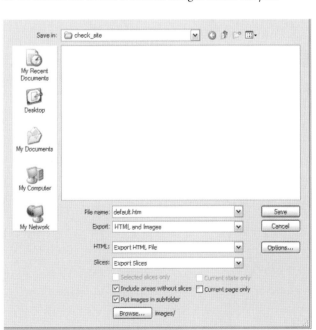

9 Click the Options button, and select the Table tab.

10 Choose Nested Tables, No Spacers from the Space With menu. This reduces the table complexity a little, but is by no means mandatory for the export.

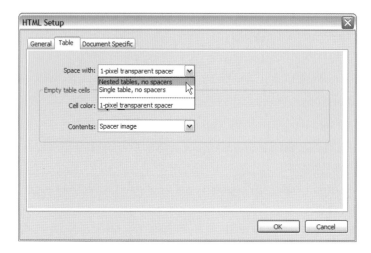

11 Click OK to close the HTML setup dialog box, and then click Save (Windows) or Export (Mac) to complete the export process.

Because this design makes use of some shared slices (the thumbnails), you will get a single prompt for each page where those slices occur, asking if you wish to overwrite the file and continue. You get this prompt because the shared slices all have the same slice names on each page.

12 When prompted to overwrite the file, click OK. This is a little tedious, but keep in mind this is just Fireworks making sure you want to overwrite an existing file. In the long run, it also reduces the number of graphics needed for the web prototype.

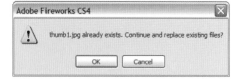

There is no progress bar for this export process, but if you try to use Fireworks while the export is occurring, it will not respond. The export process for this design should be finished within a minute or two.

13 Using Windows Explorer or the Mac Finder, locate your prototype folder.

You will see 15 web pages, including one called header.htm. That particular file is the result of exporting your master page, and is neither needed nor used for the click-through prototype. You can safely delete that from the folder.

Open the images folder and you will see a frightening number of graphics. As discussed in earlier lessons, Fireworks exports everything as graphics when you choose the Export HTML and Images option. Any areas that were not manually sliced are exported using the Fireworks auto-naming convention. Any pages containing multiple states will have images exported for each state, including ones not necessary to the design.

Again, as this is for prototyping only, it is not something you should be overly concerned about.

Feel free to double-click on the index page to launch your mockup in a web browser, and test out the links and other interactive elements.

Review questions

1 When should a master page be used?

2 How do you add new states to a page?

3 What are behaviors, and how do you apply them?

4 How do you edit JavaScript behaviors?

5 How do you turn a completed multipage Fireworks design into a clickable web prototype?

Review answers

1 You can use a master page if you have graphics that will be common to all pages, and that appear in the same pixel location on all pages.

2 You add new states by choosing New State from the States panel menu.

3 Behaviors are prebuilt JavaScript functions that can be added by clicking the behavior handle of either a hotspot or image slice object.

4 You can edit applied behaviors by opening the Behaviors panel (Window > Behaviors). Select the slice or hotspot that has the attached behaviors, and then select the specific behavior in the Behaviors panel. You can also add additional behaviors using the Behaviors panel.

5 Choose File > Export, browse to the desired directory, choose HTML and Images from the Export menu, and make sure that Include Areas Without Slices is selected and that Current Page Only is *not* selected.

INDEX

Entries for bonus supplemental chapters 12 and 13 are noted with the letter S.

B

background images, slices and, 193
backgrounds, tweaking banner ad, 128–130
banding, optimizing animation and, 226
banner ads
    adding background to, 102
    adding text to, 122–125
    creating document for, 101–102
    tweaking background of, 128–130
banner area
    navigation elements in, 273–275
    slicing, 271–272
baseline shifts, 140
batch processing, Adobe Bridge for, S:6–S:12
behavior handles, slices and, 165, 285
behaviors
    adding, 296–298
    adding rollover behaviors, 285–286
    editing JavaScript behaviors, 299–301
    what they are, 285
bitmap images
    adjusting position of, 27
    Align panel and, 33–34
    blending modes for correcting, S:38–S:43
    considerations when importing into Flash, S:89
    creating vector silhouette from, 119–121
    cropping, 25–26
    cropping individual bitmaps, S:14–S:15
    distortion-free scaling, 30–31
    Dodge and Burn tools for adjusting brightness, 36–37
    grouping objects, 34–35
    guides, working with, 28
    hiding/locking objects, 27
    importing, 28–29
    importing flattened bitmap into Flash, S:87–S:89
    lesson overview, 22
    masking, 98
    repairing areas with Rubber Stamp tool, 40–41
    resolution and file size, 24
    retouching on separate bitmap object, 41–43
    review Q & A, 44
    seamless integration with vector images, 19
    selections. *see* selections, of bitmap images
    tonal range adjustments, 32–33
    Unsharp Mask, applying as Live Filter, 38–39
    vector images compared with, 70

bitmap masks
    converting bitmap selection to mask, 114–115
    editing, 115–117
    overview of, 98–99
    vector masks compared with, 100
bitmap selection tools
    edge options, 49
    Lasso tool, 55–58
    Magic Wand tool, 50–54
    primer on use of, 48–49
Bitmap tools, of Tools panel, 10
blending modes, S:27
    Flash/Fireworks equivalents, S:81
    for image correction, S:38–S:43
bold text, Property inspector setting, 138
Bridge. *see* Adobe Bridge
brightness, adjusting with Dodge and Burn tools, 36–37
Brightness/Contrast dialog box, 128
Browse in Bridge command, S:4
Brush (B) tool
    creating bitmap masks, 98
    shortcut for, 117
Burn tool
    adjusting brightness, 36–37
    darkening with, 37
    overview of, 36
button states, adding to Flex skins, S:64
button symbols
    adding multiple buttons, 215–216
    creating, 210–212
    editing, 212–215
    overview of, 210
    rollover effects, 215

C

canvas
    customizing page dimensions, 275
    preparing, 7
    setting canvas size and color, 86
    size options in Property inspector, 219
    trimming, 224
Cascading Style Sheets. *see* CSS (Cascading Style Sheets)
case, text settings, 137
Chamfer Rectangle tool, 73
Circle Hotspot tool, 179
cloning, 41. *see also* Rubber Stamp tool

Dodge tool
    adjusting brightness, 36–37
    lightening with, 37
    overview of, 36
downsampling, 38
Drag, AIR mouse events, S:53
dragging objects, between layers, 90
drawing techniques, vector graphics, 7–8, 64
Dreamweaver
    copying and pasting to, S:67–S:72
    round trip editing, S:72–S:75
Drop Shadows, 73

E

edge options, Live Marquee, 98
Edit in Place mode, for symbol editing, 206
editing gradient colors, 103
editing masks
    bitmap masks, 115–117
    vector masks, 113
editing paths, 77
editing symbols
    button symbols, 212–215
    Edit in Place mode for, 206
    graphic symbols, 206–208
    isolation mode for, 208
editing text, 137–138
Ellipse tool, 64
events, AIR, S:48–S:53
Expand/Collapse Layer icon, 91–92
Export area tool, S:15–S:17
export options, for Photoshop, S:25–S:26
Export Wizard, Optimize panel, 155
exporting animation symbols, 228
exporting files
    PNG files as JPEG files, 162
    vs. saving files, 153
exporting Flex skins, S:65–S:66
exporting HTML and Images, 182–186
exporting prototypes, 305–307
exporting specific areas of workflow, S:15–S:17
exporting states, 187–188
exposure, Dodge and Burn tools and, 37
eXtensible Metadata Platform (XMP), S:20
eye icon, hiding objects and, 27
Eyedropper tool, 103

F

fades, Auto Vector Mask for, 106–108
feathered edge, bitmap selection tools and, 49
file size
    dither settings and, 225
    GIF animation files, 226
    images, 38
    resolution and, 24
files
    preparing for Flash, S:80–S:81
    saving for use in Photoshop, S:25–S:26
Fill Category menu, 125–126
Fill Color box, 125–126
fills
    Color Picker for filling with color, 11
    customizing, 79–81
    drawing vector shape and filling with color, 7–8
    Property inspector for setting, 68–69
filters
    applying to selections, 51
    Flash/Fireworks equivalents, S:81
Filters area, Property inspector, 32
fixed-width text blocks, 135–136
Flash, 152
    considerations when importing into Flash, S:89
    importing Fireworks documents into Flash,
        S:82–S:87
    importing flattened bitmap into, S:87–S:89
    overview of, S:80
    preparing files for, S:80–S:81
Flex skins
    adding button states, S:64
    creating, S:61–S:63
    exporting, S:65–S:66
    resources for, S:66
Flip Horizontal, transform options, 110
floating document windows
    creating, 17–18
    dragging/dropping between, 18–19
Font Style menu, Property inspector, 73
fonts
    for banner ad text, 122
    changing size of, 137
    decorative, S:33
    setting, 213
    setting size and type and weight, 72–73
    setting text attributes in Property inspector,
        134–135
    Web browsers and, 194
foreground images, slices, 193
Freeform tool, 76

symbols *(continued)*
> creating animation symbols, 218–222
> creating button symbols, 210–212
> editing button symbols, 212–215
> editing graphic symbols, 206–208
> exporting animation, 228
> graphic symbols, 200–201
> lesson overview, 199
> onion skinning animation symbols, 222–224
> optimizing animation of animation symbols, 224–226
> review Q & A, 229
> saving to Common Library, 202–203
> testing rollover effects, 216
> what they are, 200

T

templates, creating metadata template, S:22–S:23
testing rollover effects, 216
text
> adding strokes to real text, S:47
> adding strokes to rendered text, S:44–S:46
> adding to banner ad, 122–125
> adding to mockups, 217–218
> adding to vector designs, 72–73
> anti-aliasing, 141–142
> attaching to paths, 142–144
> auto-resizing, 134–135
> considerations when importing into Flash, S:89
> creating custom styles, 126–127
> CSS-based layouts and, 188
> editing, 137–138
> fixed-width text blocks, 135–136
> flowing around vector shapes, 138–140
> font and alignment settings, 213
> lesson overview, 132
> Live Filters added to, 147
> as mask, 145–146
> review Q & A, 148–149
> skewing on an angle, 144–145
> special effects, 142
> styling, 125–126
> typographic terminology and, 140

text blocks
> auto-resizing, 134–135
> fixed-width, 135–136

Text tool
> adding text to banner ad, 122
> adding text to designs, 72

creating fixed-width text blocks, 135–136
> font family settings, 213
> Property inspector attributes for, 134
texture settings, Property inspector, 68–69
three-slive technique, for content containers, S:75–S:79
Threshold property, Unsharp Mask, 39
thumbnails, size options, 93
TIFF files, adding metadata to, S:20
tonal range, 32–33
Tools panel
> 9-slice Scaling tool, 30
> accessing tool options, 11
> Dodge and Burn tools, 37
> illustration of Fireworks interface, 5
> Magic Wand tool, 50
> overview of, 10–11
> Scale tool, 30, 35
> selecting Crop tool, 25
> Skew tool, 144–145
> Transform tools, 68
> Web optimization and, 163
> Zoom tool, 28
tooltips
> making visible, 35
> shortcuts for, 7
tracking
> defined, 140
> Property inspector text attributes, 134
> setting distance between letters, 73, 217
Transform options
> Flip Horizontal, 110
> Modify menu, 35
Transform tools, 68–69
transparency settings, Web graphics, 152
transparent chrome, in AIR prototypes, S:55
typography, 140

U

Undo command, 19–20
Unsharp Mask
> applying as Live Filter, 38–39
> properties, 39
upsampling, 38
URLs, interactivity and, 179
user interface. *see* interface, getting started

workflow *(continued)*
    changing rectangle corners independently,
        S:17–S:19
    creating metadata template, S:22–S:23
    cropping individual bitmaps, S:14–S:15
    customizing Photoshop export options, S:26
    exporting specific areas, S:15–S:17
    importing images, S:12–S:13
    lesson overview, S:2
    list of Live Filters supported by Photoshop, S:27
    review Q & A, S:28
    saving files for use in Photoshop, S:25–S:26
workspace
    custom workspaces, 15–16
    default, 5
    lesson overview, 2

X

x and y coordinates
    for cursor location, 8
    symbol-editing mode and, 207
X key, for toggling between color fill and stroke,
    117
XMP (eXtensible Metadata Platform), S:20

Z

Zoom Level menu, Application Bar, 28
Zoom tool
    100% magnification, 37
    Tools panel, 28
zooming in/out of areas, S:36–S:37

Contributor

Jim Babbage teaches imaging, Web design, and photography in Toronto at Centennial College's Centre for Communication, Media, and Design (centennialcollege.ca/thecentre) and at Humber College's Digital Imaging Training Centre (digital.humber.ca). He is also a creative partner/co-owner of NewMedia Services (newmediaservices.ca), a communications company. Beginning his career as a commercial photographer, Jim started with Photoshop and then moved to web design, using early versions of Fireworks and Dreamweaver and was hooked. Jim is a frequent contributor of articles on Fireworks, Dreamweaver, Photoshop, and other general web topics to the Community MX Web site (communitymx.com) and adobe.com and has presented at Adobe MAX as well as several other conferences.

Production Notes

The *Adobe Fireworks CS4 Classroom in a Book* was created electronically using Adobe InDesign CS3. Art was produced using Adobe Photoshop. The Myriad Pro and Warnock Pro OpenType families of typefaces were used throughout this book.

References to company names in the lessons are for demonstration purposes only and are not intended to refer to any actual organization or person.

Team credits

The following individuals contributed to the development of this edition of the *Adobe Fireworks CS4 Classroom in a Book*:

Project Manager: Connie Jeung-Mills
Developmental Editor: Brie Gyncild
Production Editor: Cory Borman
Technical Editor: Derren Whiteman
Compositor: Owen Wolfson
Copyeditor: Wendy Katz
Proofreader: Liz Welch
Indexer: Jack Lewis
Cover design: Eddie Yuen
Interior design: Mimi Heft